Circular Food Economy: Advancing Food Waste Reduction, Resource Recovery, Sustainable Agriculture, Food Recycling, Circular Economy, and Resilient Food Systems

Copyright

Circular Food Economy: Advancing Food Waste Reduction, Resource Recovery, Sustainable Agriculture, Food Recycling, Circular Economy, and Resilient Food Systems

© 2025 Robert C. Brears

ISBN (eBook): 978-1-991368-17-1

ISBN (Paperback): 978-1-991368-18-8

Published by Global Climate Solutions

First Edition, 2025

Cover design and interior layout by Global Climate Solutions

Table of Contents

Introduction

The global food system stands at a crossroads, facing mounting pressures from resource scarcity, environmental degradation, population growth, and shifting consumer preferences. Traditional linear models of food production and consumption—where resources are extracted, transformed, consumed, and ultimately discarded as waste—have led to substantial inefficiencies and a range of ecological and social challenges. In response, a new paradigm is emerging: the circular food economy. This approach seeks to redesign food systems to be regenerative, resilient, and restorative, ensuring that resources are continually cycled, waste is minimized, and value is retained throughout the supply chain.

A circular food economy is characterized by its commitment to keeping resources in use for as long as possible, extracting the maximum value from them while in use, and recovering and regenerating products and materials at the end of their service life. Unlike the traditional take-make-dispose approach, circularity integrates principles such as waste prevention, resource efficiency, and the valorization of by-products. This not only addresses the environmental impacts associated with food systems—including greenhouse gas emissions, water usage, land degradation, and biodiversity loss—but also creates opportunities for economic growth, job creation, and improved food security.

The transition toward a circular food economy requires the active participation of all stakeholders, including producers, processors, retailers, consumers, policymakers, and innovators. It involves rethinking how food is produced, processed, transported, consumed, and disposed of. At its core, this transition is about transforming linear value chains into interconnected, regenerative cycles that support sustainable development. Innovative agricultural practices, new business models, digital technologies, and supportive policy frameworks are all instrumental in driving this transformation.

However, achieving a truly circular food economy is not without its challenges. Systemic barriers such as entrenched linear practices, limited access to technology and finance, regulatory constraints, and a lack of awareness can hinder progress. Overcoming these obstacles requires coordinated action at local, national, and international levels. It also necessitates a cultural shift, with individuals and organizations embracing circular thinking and adopting new behaviors.

This book provides a comprehensive exploration of the circular food economy, from foundational concepts and principles to practical strategies and enabling policies. Through detailed chapters, it examines how circularity can be applied across the entire food system—from production and processing to distribution, consumption, waste management, and resource recovery. The aim is to equip readers with the knowledge and tools needed to understand, implement, and scale circular practices for a sustainable and resilient food future.

Chapter 1: Foundations of the Circular Food Economy

The circular food economy represents a transformative shift in how food systems are designed, managed, and valued. Moving beyond the traditional linear model of "take, make, waste," circularity seeks to close resource loops, minimize waste, and regenerate natural systems. This chapter explores the foundational concepts, principles, and motivations that underpin the circular food economy. It introduces the key differences between linear and circular systems, outlines the central role of systems thinking, and highlights the diverse stakeholders and policy drivers essential for change. Together, these elements provide a roadmap for building more resilient and sustainable food systems.

Defining the Circular Food Economy

The circular food economy is a transformative approach to designing, operating, and improving food systems by closing resource loops, minimizing waste, and maximizing the value of materials, energy, and nutrients throughout the entire food value chain. Rather than viewing resources as expendable inputs and outputs, the circular food economy seeks to retain and regenerate natural capital, keep products and materials in use for as long as possible, and recover resources at the end of their service life. It challenges the prevailing linear "take-make-dispose" model, which has dominated global food systems for decades, and instead promotes an integrated, systems-based perspective focused on long-term sustainability and resilience.

At its core, the circular food economy is underpinned by three main principles: designing out waste and pollution, keeping products and materials in circulation, and regenerating natural systems. In practical terms, this means rethinking how food is produced, processed, distributed, consumed, and managed at end-of-life. By applying circular principles, food systems can shift from being major contributors to environmental problems—such as greenhouse gas emissions, water scarcity, land degradation, and loss of biodiversity—to becoming powerful drivers of regeneration, climate mitigation, and resource efficiency.

The circular food economy operates at multiple scales, from individual households and local communities to national economies and global supply chains. It involves a wide array of stakeholders— farmers, food manufacturers, retailers, consumers, waste managers, policymakers, and technology providers—each playing a unique role in closing loops and enhancing system performance. For example, farmers may implement regenerative agricultural practices that improve soil health and increase carbon sequestration; processors and manufacturers can valorize food by-products and minimize resource use; retailers can design out packaging waste and promote sustainable consumption; consumers can embrace waste reduction and resource recovery at home; and policymakers can create enabling frameworks and incentives that accelerate the adoption of circular models.

Fundamentally, the circular food economy is not just a technical or economic shift, but a cultural and societal transformation. It calls for reimagining value, rethinking relationships with food and resources, and fostering new patterns of collaboration across sectors. By embedding circularity throughout the food system, societies can reduce environmental impacts, enhance food security and nutrition, create new economic opportunities, and build resilience against shocks and stresses. In this way, the circular food economy provides a vision and pathway for achieving a sustainable, inclusive, and regenerative future for people and the planet.

Principles of Circularity in Food Systems

Circularity in food systems is guided by foundational principles that reimagine how resources are used, cycled, and renewed to achieve environmental, economic, and social sustainability. These principles provide the framework for transitioning away from linear processes toward interconnected systems that preserve value, regenerate natural capital, and minimize negative externalities.

The first core principle is designing out waste and pollution at every stage of the food system. This means addressing inefficiencies from the outset—selecting crops and livestock suited to local conditions, optimizing resource inputs, and adopting closed-loop production methods. Processing facilities can further reduce waste by maximizing the use of raw materials and minimizing the generation of by-products that cannot be reused or recycled. Packaging is designed for reuse or composting, and logistics are optimized to prevent spoilage and losses during transportation and storage.

The second principle involves keeping products and materials in use for as long as possible. This is achieved through reuse, repair, refurbishment, and recycling strategies that extend the lifecycle of food products, packaging, and inputs. Surplus food is redirected to feed people, followed by repurposing for animal feed or industrial uses, and finally processed into compost or bioenergy. By prioritizing the highest-value use for each resource, the food system becomes more resilient and less dependent on virgin materials.

Regenerating natural systems is the third foundational principle. Food systems are designed not just to minimize harm but to actively improve environmental conditions. Regenerative agriculture, agroecology, and sustainable fisheries restore soil fertility, increase biodiversity, and enhance ecosystem services such as water retention and carbon sequestration. Waste streams are transformed into valuable inputs—such as organic fertilizers or biogas—helping to replenish natural cycles and reduce reliance on synthetic alternatives.

A fourth key principle is fostering collaboration and innovation across the value chain. Stakeholders at all levels—farmers, processors, retailers, consumers, policymakers, and technology providers—work together to identify opportunities, share knowledge, and co-create solutions. Digital tools and data platforms enable transparency and traceability, making it easier to monitor resource flows and measure progress toward circularity.

Finally, circularity in food systems is grounded in the principle of equity and inclusivity. Solutions must benefit all actors in the system, ensure fair access to resources, and promote food security and nutrition for present and future generations. By adhering to these principles, food systems can shift from extractive, wasteful models to ones that nurture people, communities, and the planet.

Linear Versus Circular Food Systems

Traditional food systems are predominantly linear in design, operating under a model where natural resources are extracted, transformed into food and packaging, distributed for consumption, and ultimately disposed of as waste. This "take-make-dispose" approach has fueled significant productivity and growth but has also contributed to widespread environmental challenges, including food loss and waste, greenhouse gas emissions, water pollution, and the depletion of soils and biodiversity. In a linear system, the focus is on maximizing output and efficiency, often at the expense of long-term sustainability and resource conservation.

In contrast, circular food systems are intentionally structured to keep resources in use for as long as possible, prioritizing the continual cycling of materials and nutrients throughout the food value chain. The circular model seeks to design out waste and pollution, reuse and recycle materials, and regenerate natural systems. This means that by-products and waste streams from one stage—such as crop residues, food processing by-products, or surplus food—are viewed as valuable resources for other stages, rather than as problems to be disposed of. For example, uneaten food might be redirected to animal feed or composted to enrich soils, and packaging could be designed for reuse or recycling.

A circular approach also emphasizes regenerative practices that restore and enhance natural capital rather than depleting it.

Techniques such as regenerative agriculture, agroecology, and integrated aquaculture promote healthy soils, increase biodiversity, and sequester carbon, thus supporting ecosystem health and climate resilience. These systems are more adaptive to shocks, more efficient in resource use, and more equitable in the distribution of benefits across stakeholders.

Ultimately, the main difference lies in mindset and system design. Linear food systems prioritize short-term output and accept waste as inevitable, while circular food systems seek to redesign processes so that waste becomes a resource and value is maintained within the system. By shifting toward circularity, food systems can not only reduce their environmental footprint but also create new economic and social opportunities for a more resilient and sustainable future.

The Role of Systems Thinking

Systems thinking is fundamental to understanding and advancing circularity within food systems. Unlike traditional approaches that focus on isolated components or single stages of the value chain, systems thinking considers the interconnections, feedback loops, and dependencies that shape the overall functioning of the food system. It recognizes that food production, processing, distribution, consumption, and waste management are all deeply linked, with changes in one area often having ripple effects throughout the entire system.

Applying systems thinking means mapping the flow of materials, energy, and nutrients across the food value chain and identifying points where inefficiencies, losses, or environmental impacts occur. It encourages a holistic view that accounts for social, economic, and environmental dimensions, as well as the roles played by different actors such as farmers, manufacturers, retailers, consumers, and policymakers. This approach enables the identification of leverage points—critical stages or interactions where targeted interventions can lead to significant improvements in circularity and sustainability.

Systems thinking also highlights the importance of feedback mechanisms and adaptive management. By monitoring outcomes and flows in real time, stakeholders can adjust practices and policies to respond to changing conditions, emerging challenges, or new opportunities. For example, real-time data collection can help food businesses reduce waste, optimize supply chains, and develop more responsive distribution networks.

Furthermore, systems thinking fosters cross-sector collaboration and innovation. When stakeholders recognize their mutual interdependence, they are more likely to partner on solutions that benefit the entire system—such as developing platforms for surplus food redistribution, coordinating on packaging reuse, or investing in shared resource recovery infrastructure.

By adopting systems thinking, those involved in the food economy can move beyond piecemeal fixes and design integrated strategies that address root causes of waste, inefficiency, and resource depletion. This mindset supports the transition from linear to circular models, building food systems that are more resilient, adaptive, and capable of sustaining both people and the environment over the long term.

Key Stakeholders and Their Roles

The transition to a circular food economy requires coordinated action from a diverse array of stakeholders, each playing a distinct and essential role in redesigning and sustaining circular practices across the food system. Understanding the contributions and responsibilities of these stakeholders is crucial for achieving meaningful change and building resilient, resource-efficient food systems.

Farmers and primary producers are at the forefront, as their decisions regarding crop selection, soil management, input use, and livestock practices set the foundation for resource flows and environmental impacts throughout the system. By adopting regenerative and circular approaches—such as crop rotation, agroecology, and on-farm waste valorization—they can significantly reduce resource inputs and close nutrient loops.

Food processors and manufacturers influence how raw agricultural products are transformed, packaged, and prepared for market. They have opportunities to minimize waste, recover by-products, and invest in eco-design and resource-efficient technologies. Their procurement strategies and partnerships with suppliers can drive the adoption of circular principles upstream in the supply chain.

Retailers and distributors connect producers with consumers and play a pivotal role in shaping how food is presented, marketed, and delivered. Through inventory management, sustainable sourcing policies, and innovations in packaging and logistics, they can reduce losses and facilitate the recovery and redistribution of surplus food.

Consumers are both end-users and active participants in the circular food economy. Their purchasing decisions, food preparation habits, and willingness to embrace new products or practices—such as food sharing, composting, or using reusable packaging—influence demand for circular solutions. Public awareness campaigns and education can empower consumers to make choices that align with circularity goals.

Waste managers and resource recovery organizations close the loop by collecting, processing, and repurposing food waste, packaging, and other by-products. Their expertise in composting, anaerobic digestion, recycling, and bioproduct development ensures that valuable materials are returned to productive use rather than sent to landfill.

Policymakers and regulators create enabling environments by setting standards, incentives, and regulations that encourage circular practices across the food system. Their leadership is vital for driving systemic change, fostering innovation, and addressing barriers such as market failures or regulatory gaps.

Technology providers and innovators support all stakeholders by developing tools for traceability, process optimization, and waste reduction. Digital platforms, sensors, and data analytics facilitate transparency and collaboration.

Collaboration among these stakeholders is essential for scaling solutions, sharing knowledge, and integrating circularity at every stage of the food system. Only through collective action can the vision of a circular food economy become a reality.

Policy Drivers and Global Initiatives

Policy frameworks and global initiatives play a pivotal role in accelerating the transition to a circular food economy. Governments, international organizations, and industry coalitions are increasingly recognizing the need to move beyond linear, resource-intensive food systems and are implementing policies and programs to promote circularity, sustainability, and resource efficiency.

At the national level, policy drivers include regulations that encourage waste prevention, resource recovery, and sustainable production practices. Governments may introduce targets for reducing food loss and waste, provide incentives for composting and recycling, or set standards for eco-friendly packaging. Subsidies and grants can support farmers and businesses in adopting regenerative agriculture, investing in circular technologies, or developing infrastructure for resource recovery. Fiscal measures, such as landfill taxes or extended producer responsibility schemes, further incentivize the reduction and valorization of waste throughout the food value chain.

Globally, international agreements and strategies help align countries and stakeholders around common goals. The United Nations Sustainable Development Goals (SDGs), particularly Goal 12 (Responsible Consumption and Production), serve as a guiding framework for efforts to make food systems more circular and sustainable. The European Union's Circular Economy Action Plan and Farm to Fork Strategy exemplify regional policy leadership by setting ambitious targets for food waste reduction, sustainable agriculture, and circular business models. Other countries and regions have developed their own roadmaps, action plans, and coalitions to foster innovation and collaboration in the circular economy.

Multilateral organizations, such as the Food and Agriculture Organization (FAO), the United Nations Environment Programme (UNEP), and the World Bank, support knowledge sharing, capacity building, and investment in circular food systems. Initiatives like the Champions 12.3 coalition, the Ellen MacArthur Foundation's Food Initiative, and the Global Alliance for Circular Economy and Resource Efficiency (GACERE) bring together governments, businesses, researchers, and civil society to share best practices, set ambitious commitments, and accelerate progress.

These policy drivers and initiatives foster enabling environments where stakeholders can experiment with new approaches, access funding and technical support, and scale up successful models. As momentum for circularity grows, continued leadership and collaboration at all levels—local, national, and international—will be crucial for transforming food systems and achieving long-term sustainability goals.

Barriers and Opportunities for Transition

The shift from linear to circular food systems presents both significant barriers and compelling opportunities. Recognizing and addressing these factors is essential for unlocking the full potential of a circular food economy.

One of the primary barriers is the persistence of entrenched linear practices throughout the food value chain. Established habits, business models, and infrastructure are often designed for efficiency and scale, rather than circularity. Many producers and companies face financial and operational risks when investing in new processes, equipment, or technologies that support circularity, particularly when short-term returns are uncertain. In addition, limited access to capital and lack of technical know-how can impede the adoption of circular approaches, especially for smallholders and smaller enterprises.

Regulatory and policy environments can also hinder progress. Existing regulations may not recognize or incentivize circular solutions such as food upcycling, resource recovery, or composting, and may instead reinforce linear models through subsidies or waste disposal practices. Inconsistent policies across jurisdictions can create confusion and complexity for businesses operating in multiple markets.

Consumer awareness and behavior represent another key challenge. Many consumers are unfamiliar with the concept of circularity or uncertain about how to participate in circular food systems. Changing purchasing and disposal habits requires sustained education, engagement, and the development of convenient, accessible solutions.

Despite these barriers, the transition to a circular food economy is rich with opportunities. Circular models can generate cost savings, reduce environmental impacts, and create new revenue streams from by-products and waste valorization. Regenerative agriculture, closed-loop processing, and resource recovery can enhance food security, support rural livelihoods, and improve ecosystem health.

Technological innovation is opening new pathways for circularity, from digital platforms that match surplus food with recipients, to advanced composting and bioconversion solutions. Collaboration across the value chain enables stakeholders to share risks, pool resources, and scale up successful initiatives. Policymakers are increasingly providing incentives, funding, and supportive regulatory frameworks to accelerate the adoption of circular practices.

Overall, the challenges of transitioning to a circular food economy can be overcome through coordinated action, innovation, and leadership. By addressing barriers and seizing emerging opportunities, stakeholders can build food systems that are more sustainable, resilient, and aligned with the needs of both people and the planet.

Chapter 2: Circular Design in Food Production

Circular design in food production reimagines how resources are used, conserved, and renewed from the very beginning of the food value chain. This chapter examines the core strategies and innovations that enable agriculture and food production systems to minimize waste, maximize resource efficiency, and enhance ecosystem health. Through regenerative practices, crop diversification, sustainable livestock and aquaculture, and advanced input management, circular design transforms food production into a driver of sustainability. The chapter provides an in-depth look at how these practices lay the groundwork for food systems that are both productive and restorative.

Designing Out Waste in Agriculture

Designing out waste in agriculture is a cornerstone of the circular food economy, aiming to prevent the generation of waste at every stage of food production. This approach shifts the focus from managing waste after it occurs to proactively minimizing its creation through better design, planning, and operational strategies. By adopting circular principles, agriculture can become more resource-efficient, resilient, and sustainable.

A central strategy for designing out waste is optimizing input use. Farmers can reduce the need for synthetic fertilizers and pesticides by employing precision agriculture, crop rotation, and integrated pest management. These methods ensure that inputs are used only where and when they are needed, reducing excess application and minimizing runoff or leaching into the environment. Advanced irrigation systems, such as drip or sensor-based technologies, help conserve water and reduce losses due to evaporation or overuse.

Another important tactic involves maximizing the use of all outputs from agricultural activities. Crop residues, such as stalks, leaves, and husks, can be collected and repurposed for animal feed, compost, bioenergy, or soil amendments rather than being burned or discarded. Livestock manure and other organic wastes can be processed into valuable products like biogas or organic fertilizers, closing nutrient cycles and reducing dependence on external inputs.

Diversification of crops and the integration of mixed farming systems also play a role in reducing waste. By cultivating a variety of crops and incorporating livestock or agroforestry elements, farmers can create more resilient systems that make full use of available resources and reduce vulnerability to pests, diseases, and market fluctuations. Mixed systems enable the use of by-products from one activity as inputs for another, promoting resource circularity.

Collaboration across the value chain is essential for designing out waste. Farmers, processors, and technology providers can work together to develop solutions for harvesting, storage, and transport that minimize losses. Data sharing and digital tools enable better forecasting, inventory management, and coordination, ensuring that perishable goods are used efficiently and reach markets in optimal condition.

Through thoughtful design and the integration of circular practices, agriculture can drastically reduce waste, improve productivity, and contribute to the overall sustainability of food systems. This proactive approach not only conserves valuable resources but also generates new opportunities for value creation in the agricultural sector.

Regenerative Agricultural Practices

Regenerative agricultural practices are a vital component of the circular food economy, focusing on restoring and enhancing the health of ecosystems while producing food. Unlike conventional approaches that often degrade soil, water, and biodiversity, regenerative agriculture aims to build natural capital and foster long-term sustainability. This approach works with nature rather than against it, resulting in resilient systems that support productive agriculture and environmental regeneration.

At the core of regenerative agriculture is the improvement of soil health. Practices such as cover cropping, reduced tillage, and the use of organic amendments enrich soil organic matter, improve structure, and enhance water retention. Healthy soils can better withstand droughts and floods, support beneficial soil organisms, and store more carbon, thereby contributing to climate change mitigation. By minimizing soil disturbance and promoting continuous plant cover, regenerative farmers reduce erosion and maintain nutrient cycles.

Crop rotation and polyculture are key techniques for boosting system diversity and resilience. Alternating different crops in the same field disrupts pest and disease cycles, reducing the need for chemical interventions. Integrating a variety of plant species through intercropping or agroforestry further increases ecosystem complexity, supports pollinators and other beneficial organisms, and enhances overall system productivity. These diverse systems make efficient use of available nutrients and sunlight, reducing waste and input requirements.

Regenerative livestock management also contributes to circularity. Adaptive grazing techniques, where animals are rotated across pastures, prevent overgrazing, allow grasslands to recover, and stimulate plant growth. Livestock can be integrated into cropping systems to consume crop residues and provide manure, which acts as a valuable organic fertilizer. This closed-loop approach returns nutrients to the soil, reduces the need for synthetic inputs, and improves pasture health.

Water management is another critical aspect of regenerative agriculture. Techniques such as contour plowing, the creation of swales, and the restoration of wetlands help manage water flows across the landscape, reduce runoff, and increase groundwater recharge. These practices support resilient water cycles and protect against drought and flooding, while also enhancing local biodiversity.

Community engagement and farmer knowledge sharing are essential for scaling regenerative practices. Peer-to-peer networks, cooperative models, and partnerships with research institutions enable the exchange of experiences, access to resources, and the adaptation of techniques to local conditions. Policymakers and supply chain actors can further support regenerative agriculture through incentives, market access, and recognition of ecosystem services.

Through the adoption of regenerative agricultural practices, food systems can move beyond sustainability to actively improve ecosystems, sequester carbon, enhance biodiversity, and build long-term resilience. This approach not only benefits the environment but also strengthens farm productivity and rural livelihoods, creating a more circular and regenerative food economy.

Crop Diversification and Resilient Food Systems

Crop diversification is a foundational strategy for building resilient food systems within the framework of a circular food economy. By cultivating a range of crops instead of relying on monocultures, farmers can spread risks, make more efficient use of resources, and enhance the health and stability of agroecosystems. This approach increases the capacity of food systems to withstand shocks from pests, diseases, climate extremes, and market fluctuations, ensuring more reliable food production over time.

Diversified cropping systems contribute to soil health and fertility by interrupting pest and disease cycles and reducing dependency on chemical inputs. Rotating crops with different nutrient requirements and rooting patterns helps maintain balanced soil nutrition, prevent depletion of specific nutrients, and reduce the buildup of pathogens and pests. Including legumes in rotations, for example, enriches the soil with nitrogen, lessening the need for synthetic fertilizers and supporting subsequent crops.

Integrating a variety of crops also supports biodiversity, both above and below ground. Polyculture systems—where multiple species are grown together—create complex habitats for beneficial insects, pollinators, and soil organisms, contributing to ecosystem stability and natural pest regulation. Agroforestry systems, which combine crops with trees or shrubs, offer additional benefits such as shade, wind protection, and improved microclimates, while producing a wider array of products including fruits, nuts, timber, and medicinal plants.

From an economic perspective, crop diversification can buffer farmers against price volatility and crop failures. By growing multiple crops with different market windows and uses, producers have more consistent income streams and greater flexibility to respond to changing market demands. Diversified production systems are also better positioned to supply local and regional food markets, supporting food security and community resilience.

Crop diversification aligns closely with circularity by encouraging the use of on-farm resources, reducing waste, and maximizing the value generated from each hectare of land. Residues from one crop can be used as mulch, animal feed, or compost for others, creating synergies and closing resource loops. By designing systems that mimic natural diversity, farmers foster resilience, enhance productivity, and build the foundation for sustainable, circular food systems capable of meeting the challenges of a changing world.

Sustainable Livestock and Aquaculture

Sustainable livestock and aquaculture systems are integral to the circular food economy, providing protein and other valuable products while promoting efficient resource use and minimizing environmental impacts. These systems prioritize the responsible management of animals and aquatic species, aiming to align food production with ecological principles and circularity goals.

In livestock production, sustainable practices focus on optimizing feed efficiency, managing manure as a resource, and integrating animals within broader agroecological systems. By adopting rotational grazing and mixed-species grazing, farmers can enhance pasture health, reduce soil erosion, and promote plant diversity. Manure is not treated as waste but rather as a valuable input for soil fertility, returning nutrients to fields and closing nutrient loops. Sustainable feed strategies include sourcing local or by-product feeds, reducing reliance on imported grains, and utilizing crop residues, further embedding livestock within the circular flow of resources.

Aquaculture systems can also contribute to circularity when designed with resource recovery and ecosystem health in mind. Integrated multi-trophic aquaculture (IMTA), for example, cultivates complementary species—such as fish, shellfish, and seaweeds— together. Waste from one species becomes food or fertilizer for another, improving water quality and maximizing output with minimal external inputs. Land-based aquaculture can harness recirculating water systems to reduce freshwater use and recover nutrients for use in agriculture or horticulture.

Both livestock and aquaculture sectors benefit from innovations in waste management and resource efficiency. Anaerobic digestion of manure and fish waste produces biogas for energy and nutrient-rich digestate for use as fertilizer. Technologies for recovering proteins, fats, and other valuable compounds from processing by-products add further value and reduce environmental burdens.

Animal welfare is a critical component of sustainability. Humane treatment and good husbandry practices not only improve productivity and product quality but also align with consumer expectations and ethical standards. Disease prevention through good management, biosecurity, and vaccination reduces the need for antibiotics and chemicals, supporting ecosystem and human health.

Sustainable livestock and aquaculture systems close resource loops, support rural livelihoods, and contribute to food security. By integrating circular principles—resource recovery, waste minimization, and ecosystem stewardship—these sectors help build resilient, productive, and environmentally sound food systems for the future.

Input Efficiency: Water, Energy, and Fertilizers

Enhancing input efficiency is essential for advancing a circular food economy, as it reduces resource consumption, lowers costs, and minimizes environmental impacts throughout the agricultural value chain. The efficient use of water, energy, and fertilizers not only conserves scarce resources but also strengthens the resilience and productivity of farming systems.

Water efficiency in agriculture is achieved through a combination of improved irrigation technologies, better crop selection, and smart water management practices. Techniques such as drip irrigation, sprinkler systems, and soil moisture sensors ensure that water is applied precisely where and when it is needed, minimizing losses from evaporation, runoff, and overwatering. Rainwater harvesting and the reuse of treated wastewater further supplement water supplies and reduce the pressure on freshwater sources. Matching crops to local climate and soil conditions also enhances water productivity, as some species are naturally more water-efficient than others.

Energy efficiency is another pillar of circular agriculture. The adoption of renewable energy sources—such as solar, wind, or biogas generated from farm waste—reduces dependency on fossil fuels and cuts greenhouse gas emissions. Optimizing field operations, using energy-efficient equipment, and scheduling activities to take advantage of off-peak power further decrease energy consumption. Integrating energy and nutrient flows, for example by using waste heat from greenhouses or digesters to warm buildings or water, creates synergies and boosts overall system efficiency.

Fertilizer efficiency involves using nutrients wisely to maximize crop uptake while minimizing losses to the environment. Precision agriculture tools, including GPS-guided machinery and remote sensing technologies, enable site-specific application of fertilizers based on real-time crop needs. Incorporating organic fertilizers such as compost, manure, or digestate from biogas production reduces reliance on synthetic inputs and helps close nutrient cycles. Cover cropping, crop rotation, and intercropping with legumes also naturally improve soil fertility and reduce the need for external fertilizers.

By focusing on input efficiency, farmers and food producers reduce their environmental footprint, improve profitability, and create more resilient systems. These efficiency gains are central to circular food economies, as they support the sustainable intensification of production, ensure the responsible use of resources, and promote the regeneration of natural capital for future generations.

Technology and Innovation in Circular Production

Technology and innovation are driving forces behind the transformation of conventional agriculture into circular production systems. By leveraging advanced tools, digital solutions, and process innovations, food producers can optimize resource use, minimize waste, and create new value from previously underutilized materials.

Digital technologies such as remote sensing, satellite imagery, and drones provide real-time data on crop health, soil moisture, and field conditions. This information enables precision agriculture, allowing farmers to apply water, fertilizers, and pesticides only where needed and in the exact amounts required. As a result, resource efficiency is improved, environmental impacts are reduced, and yields are optimized.

Sensors and automated systems facilitate continuous monitoring and management of production environments, from greenhouses to open fields. Internet of Things (IoT) devices track inputs and outputs, support traceability, and alert farmers to potential problems before they become critical, enabling proactive intervention and reducing waste. Blockchain technology offers secure and transparent recordkeeping across the supply chain, supporting accountability and circularity through verifiable tracking of resource flows.

Innovative processing technologies further enhance circularity in production. On-farm biorefineries can convert crop residues, livestock manure, and other by-products into bioenergy, biofertilizers, and high-value bioproducts, creating additional income streams while reducing waste disposal needs. Closed-loop water recycling systems capture, treat, and reuse water within production facilities, minimizing freshwater use and nutrient loss.

Advances in plant breeding and biotechnology contribute to the development of resilient crop varieties with improved nutrient uptake, pest resistance, and adaptability to changing climates. These innovations support sustainable production with fewer external inputs and less risk of crop failure.

Collaboration platforms and knowledge-sharing networks connect farmers, researchers, and industry partners, accelerating the adoption of best practices and new technologies. By embracing technology and innovation, circular production systems become more adaptive, efficient, and capable of delivering both economic and environmental benefits. This continual evolution is essential for scaling up circular practices and achieving the transformation of food systems toward long-term sustainability.

Collaboration and Partnerships in Circular Production

Collaboration and partnerships are essential to advancing circular production within food systems. No single actor can achieve a fully circular model alone; effective change relies on coordinated efforts across the value chain, linking farmers, agribusinesses, researchers, technology providers, policymakers, and civil society.

Multi-stakeholder partnerships foster the exchange of knowledge, resources, and expertise. By working together, farmers can access new technologies, participate in cooperative purchasing, and share best practices that drive resource efficiency and waste reduction. Partnerships between agricultural producers and food processors enable the valorization of by-products, as surplus or residual materials from farms can be transformed into new products, bioenergy, or soil amendments through innovative processing solutions.

Collaboration with technology providers introduces digital tools, automation, and precision equipment that optimize resource use and improve system transparency. Academic and research institutions contribute by developing and disseminating cutting-edge approaches for sustainable production, tailored to local needs and conditions.

Public-private partnerships play a key role in scaling circular production. Governments and development agencies can provide financial incentives, technical support, and enabling policy frameworks, while private sector actors invest in infrastructure, market development, and supply chain integration. These joint efforts lower barriers to adoption and help build resilient, regionally adapted circular production networks.

Engaging civil society organizations and consumer groups ensures that circular initiatives are aligned with community needs and values. Education campaigns and participatory projects encourage widespread adoption and reinforce circular behaviors throughout the food system.

Through active collaboration and the formation of strategic partnerships, stakeholders pool resources, spread risk, and accelerate the transition to circular production. These collective actions enhance the effectiveness and reach of circular solutions, creating resilient, inclusive, and sustainable food systems that deliver shared value for all participants.

Chapter 3: Sustainable Food Processing and Manufacturing

Sustainable food processing and manufacturing are vital pillars of the circular food economy, ensuring that value is preserved and waste minimized as food moves from farm to table. This chapter explores how innovative technologies, resource-efficient practices, and process redesigns can transform traditional manufacturing into closed-loop systems. Key topics include reducing input and resource use, valorizing by-products, recovering water and energy, and harnessing digital tools for greater transparency and traceability. By embedding circularity at the heart of food processing, the sector can support sustainability, reduce environmental impact, and contribute to resilient, future-ready food systems.

Minimizing Resource Use in Processing

Minimizing resource use in food processing is a critical aspect of building a circular food economy. Processing facilities, which transform raw agricultural products into food items, beverages, and ingredients, are significant users of water, energy, and materials. By adopting resource-efficient practices and technologies, the food processing sector can substantially reduce its environmental footprint while supporting economic and operational resilience.

Resource minimization begins with optimizing the design and layout of processing plants. Facilities can be engineered to reduce energy and water requirements by implementing efficient production lines, using heat recovery systems, and installing energy-saving lighting and equipment. Upgrading to modern machinery with higher efficiency ratings, automating production processes, and maintaining regular equipment servicing all contribute to reduced energy consumption and lower operational costs.

Water use is another area where significant reductions can be made. Implementing closed-loop water systems, where water is treated and reused multiple times within the facility, reduces the demand for fresh water and decreases wastewater generation. Technologies such as membrane filtration, reverse osmosis, and ultraviolet disinfection enable the safe and efficient reuse of water in cleaning, cooling, and other non-product contact applications. Monitoring water use with sensors and real-time data systems allows for quick identification and rectification of leaks or inefficiencies.

Raw material efficiency is equally important. By maximizing yield from each input and minimizing waste at every stage, processors can make better use of agricultural produce. Techniques such as automated sorting, precision cutting, and optimized batch processing reduce the volume of trimmings and rejects. Surplus or by-product materials can be captured for use in animal feed, biogas generation, or further processing into value-added products.

Packaging innovations further support resource minimization. Lightweight, recyclable, or compostable packaging materials reduce material input and end-of-life waste. Right-sizing packaging to product needs prevents overuse and facilitates more efficient transport and storage.

Employee engagement and training also play a key role. Empowering staff to identify resource-saving opportunities and implement best practices ensures continuous improvement.

By prioritizing the efficient use of water, energy, and raw materials, food processors contribute to a circular economy that values resources, reduces waste, and delivers both environmental and economic benefits. These efforts help create a more sustainable food system capable of meeting present and future demands.

Eco-Design and Packaging Solutions

Eco-design and innovative packaging solutions are central to the transition toward a circular food economy, as they address both the environmental impact and resource efficiency of food systems. The goal of eco-design is to minimize waste and environmental harm by considering the entire lifecycle of packaging materials, from sourcing and manufacturing to use and end-of-life management.

One key strategy is the selection of sustainable, renewable, or recycled materials. Packaging made from plant-based bioplastics, recycled paper, or compostable fibers reduces dependency on virgin materials and supports the creation of closed-loop systems. The use of mono-materials—packaging composed of a single type of material—simplifies recycling processes and increases the likelihood that packaging will be effectively recovered and reused.

Designing for reuse and multiple life cycles is another important aspect of eco-design. Refillable containers, returnable glass bottles, and durable crates can be collected, cleaned, and reintroduced into circulation, decreasing the demand for single-use items. Systems that encourage consumers to return packaging—such as deposit-refund schemes or reverse logistics—help ensure that materials remain within the supply chain and are less likely to end up as litter or landfill.

Right-sizing and lightweighting packaging reduces material consumption and transportation impacts. Custom-designed packaging that fits products precisely eliminates unnecessary bulk, leading to lower resource use during production and more efficient distribution. These innovations also help maintain product quality by minimizing damage and spoilage during handling and transit.

Advancements in smart and active packaging offer additional environmental benefits. Technologies that extend shelf life, monitor freshness, or provide real-time information on storage conditions support better inventory management and reduce food waste. Packaging can also be labeled with clear instructions for recycling or composting, making it easier for consumers to dispose of it responsibly.

Collaboration across the value chain is critical for scaling eco-design and packaging solutions. Food producers, manufacturers, retailers, and recyclers must work together to standardize materials, establish collection systems, and invest in recycling infrastructure. Policymakers can support these efforts by setting targets, offering incentives, and enforcing regulations that encourage sustainable packaging design and responsible material management. Through ongoing innovation and partnership, food systems can move closer to circularity and reduce their environmental impact.

Valorization of Food By-Products and Side Streams

Valorization of food by-products and side streams is a core principle of the circular food economy, transforming what would traditionally be considered waste into valuable resources for new applications. This approach closes resource loops, maximizes the value extracted from raw materials, and minimizes the environmental burden of food processing and manufacturing.

By-products and side streams arise at every stage of the food value chain, from field to factory. Examples include fruit and vegetable peels, pulp, bran, whey, spent grains, shells, and trimmings. Instead of discarding these materials, innovative processing methods can convert them into a range of products with nutritional, industrial, or energy value. For instance, fruit peels and vegetable trimmings can be processed into animal feed, natural flavorings, or dietary fiber ingredients. Cereal bran and spent grains serve as raw materials for high-fiber foods, fermentation substrates, or bio-based plastics.

Biochemical and physical technologies play an important role in unlocking the potential of by-products. Enzymatic treatments, fermentation, and extraction methods can separate proteins, oils, antioxidants, and other valuable compounds from side streams. These extracted substances find use in the production of functional foods, supplements, cosmetics, or pharmaceuticals. In some cases, by-products are used to produce biogas or bioethanol, providing renewable energy while reducing landfill disposal.

The valorization process is not limited to large-scale operations. Small and medium enterprises, cooperatives, and community-based initiatives can participate in resource recovery and the creation of local value chains. The development of markets for secondary products encourages innovation and entrepreneurship, providing new income opportunities for farmers and processors.

Policy frameworks and industry standards are key to supporting valorization. Food safety regulations, quality standards, and labeling requirements help ensure that by-product-derived products are safe and accepted by consumers. Investment in research, technology transfer, and collaboration among stakeholders further enables the scaling of valorization initiatives.

A focus on valorization shifts perceptions around food system waste, recognizing it as a resource with the potential to deliver nutritional, economic, and environmental benefits. As more businesses and communities adopt these practices, circular food systems become increasingly efficient, innovative, and sustainable.

Wastewater and Energy Recovery in Processing

Wastewater and energy recovery are essential elements in making food processing operations more circular and sustainable. Processing facilities generate significant volumes of wastewater and consume large amounts of energy, often resulting in resource losses and environmental impacts. By adopting recovery and reuse strategies, these facilities can reduce their dependence on fresh inputs, lower operational costs, and mitigate pollution.

Modern wastewater treatment technologies enable the recovery of water, nutrients, and energy from processing effluents. Systems such as membrane filtration, anaerobic digesters, and advanced oxidation processes remove contaminants and pathogens, allowing water to be reused within the facility for cleaning, cooling, or even in certain production processes. This internal recycling decreases demand for external water sources and reduces the volume of wastewater that must be discharged or treated off-site.

In addition to water recovery, the organic content of wastewater and processing by-products can be harnessed for energy generation. Anaerobic digestion breaks down organic matter in effluents and solid wastes, producing biogas that can be used for heating, electricity generation, or as a fuel for facility vehicles. This not only diverts waste from landfill but also provides a renewable energy source, contributing to reduced greenhouse gas emissions.

Heat recovery is another strategy for improving energy efficiency in processing plants. Excess heat generated from cooking, pasteurization, or refrigeration can be captured and redirected to preheat water, warm buildings, or support other thermal processes. This reduces the need for additional energy inputs and enhances overall system efficiency.

The integration of wastewater and energy recovery solutions often requires cross-departmental collaboration, investment in new technologies, and ongoing monitoring. Staff training, routine maintenance, and data analytics support continuous improvement and maximize recovery potential.

Facilities that prioritize recovery of water, nutrients, and energy demonstrate leadership in circular economy principles. Such practices support operational resilience, regulatory compliance, and a reduced environmental footprint, helping food processors align with broader sustainability goals.

Digitalization for Transparency and Traceability

Digitalization is transforming food processing by enabling greater transparency and traceability throughout the supply chain. The adoption of digital tools, data platforms, and advanced analytics makes it possible to monitor, record, and verify resource flows, production processes, and product movements in real time. This shift supports the principles of a circular food economy by ensuring that information about inputs, outputs, and by-products is accurate, accessible, and actionable.

IoT devices, sensors, and cloud-based management systems play a central role in gathering data from across processing facilities. These technologies track everything from raw material sourcing and inventory levels to energy consumption and waste generation. Automated data collection reduces errors, saves time, and creates a digital record that can be analyzed for patterns, inefficiencies, or areas for improvement.

Blockchain technology is increasingly being used to secure and share data across the food value chain. By creating tamper-proof, decentralized records, blockchain allows stakeholders to trace products back to their origin, verify sustainability claims, and ensure compliance with safety and quality standards. This level of traceability is particularly valuable for circular food systems, where verifying the source, composition, and treatment of materials is crucial for building trust among consumers and regulators.

Transparency extends to sharing information with consumers and partners. Digital labeling, QR codes, and interactive platforms provide end-users with detailed insights about a product's lifecycle, ingredients, and environmental impact. This fosters informed purchasing decisions and strengthens the credibility of circular initiatives.

Digitalization also streamlines supply chain coordination, supporting real-time communication among producers, processors, distributors, and retailers. It enables rapid responses to disruptions, better demand forecasting, and more efficient resource allocation, which collectively reduce waste and enhance system resilience.

Embracing digitalization for transparency and traceability not only improves operational efficiency but also aligns food processing with the ethical and sustainability expectations of modern markets. These tools are foundational for scaling circular practices and fostering accountability throughout the food system.

Integrating Circularity in Supply Chains

Integrating circularity into food supply chains is essential for advancing sustainable production and consumption. A circular supply chain rethinks every link in the chain—sourcing, processing, packaging, distribution, and end-of-life management—to prioritize resource efficiency, minimize waste, and extend the life of materials and products.

Circular supply chains begin with responsible sourcing. This involves selecting raw materials that are renewable, recycled, or sustainably produced, and building relationships with suppliers who follow circular principles. Procurement policies may favor suppliers who demonstrate reduced environmental footprints or who participate in closed-loop initiatives, such as returning packaging or using by-products as feedstocks.

During processing and packaging, circularity is enhanced by maximizing the use of all inputs and minimizing the generation of waste. By-products and surplus materials are repurposed into new products or redirected for animal feed, compost, or bioenergy. Packaging design focuses on materials that are recyclable, reusable, or compostable, and on reducing unnecessary packaging wherever possible.

Distribution systems are optimized to reduce losses and improve efficiency. Innovations in logistics—such as shared transport, route optimization, and temperature-controlled storage—help maintain product quality, reduce spoilage, and lower energy use. Digital tracking tools and real-time data sharing provide transparency, enabling more responsive and coordinated supply chain management.

Reverse logistics is a defining feature of circular supply chains. Systems are established to collect used packaging, unsold food, or surplus products from retailers and consumers. These materials are then reintegrated into the supply chain for reuse, recycling, or upcycling, reducing the need for new inputs and diverting materials from landfill.

Engaging all stakeholders is critical for successful integration of circularity. Collaboration between producers, manufacturers, distributors, retailers, and end-users ensures that materials flow efficiently and that circular practices are upheld throughout the chain. Training, incentives, and clear communication help align goals and expectations, making it easier to scale up circular initiatives.

Integrating circularity in supply chains also prepares businesses to comply with emerging regulations and meet consumer demand for sustainable products. Supply chains that embrace circular principles are more resilient to disruptions, reduce operational risks, and unlock new sources of value through innovation and resource recovery. This holistic approach positions food systems for long-term sustainability and competitiveness in a changing global landscape.

Scaling Sustainable Processing: Challenges and Solutions

Scaling sustainable processing within the food sector presents a unique set of challenges, but also opens pathways to meaningful transformation. Processing facilities must move beyond incremental improvements to embrace systemic changes that support resource efficiency, waste minimization, and the integration of circular principles at every stage of production.

One major challenge is the high initial investment required for new technologies and process upgrades. Modernizing equipment, implementing closed-loop water and energy systems, and adopting innovative waste valorization solutions often demand significant capital outlays. Small and medium-sized enterprises may find these investments particularly difficult without access to external funding, financial incentives, or partnerships.

Operational complexity is another barrier. Sustainable processing requires changes in facility design, staff training, monitoring systems, and management practices. Integrating new technologies—such as sensors, automation, or real-time analytics—can disrupt existing workflows and require specialized expertise. Change management and capacity building are essential to ensure that teams understand, accept, and can operate new systems effectively.

Regulatory compliance adds a further layer of complexity. Food safety standards, waste management regulations, and reporting requirements can vary widely across regions. Navigating these standards while pursuing circularity demands careful coordination and often, ongoing dialogue with regulators.

Market dynamics can also affect the pace of adoption. Demand for sustainably processed products must be cultivated through consumer education, clear labeling, and strong communication of environmental and health benefits. Without sufficient market pull, companies may be reluctant to invest in or scale up circular processing solutions.

Despite these challenges, several solutions are emerging to support the scaling of sustainable processing. Collaborative partnerships—between companies, research institutions, technology providers, and government agencies—can pool resources, share risk, and accelerate innovation. Access to green financing, grants, and policy incentives helps reduce the financial burden of adoption and rewards early movers.

Investment in workforce development, ongoing training, and knowledge-sharing platforms builds the skills needed to manage new technologies and processes. Digitalization streamlines operations and enables precise resource tracking, making it easier to identify and act on improvement opportunities.

Addressing these challenges through coordinated effort, investment, and innovation supports the scaling of sustainable processing, ensuring food systems can meet environmental, social, and economic goals in a circular economy.

Chapter 4: Circular Food Distribution and Retail

Circular food distribution and retail redefine how food is transported, presented, and made available to consumers, emphasizing efficiency, sustainability, and waste reduction. This chapter investigates innovative logistics, sustainable packaging, and inventory management strategies that support circularity throughout the supply chain. It also highlights the role of collaboration among distributors, retailers, and consumers in minimizing losses, promoting resource recovery, and enabling circular business models. By transforming distribution and retail operations, food systems can better align with circular principles, reduce their environmental footprint, and meet the growing demand for sustainable choices.

Reducing Losses in Distribution Networks

Reducing losses in distribution networks is a vital strategy for building a circular food economy and improving the efficiency and resilience of food systems. Losses during distribution—whether from spoilage, mishandling, or inefficiencies—represent a significant waste of resources, energy, and labor. Addressing these losses not only conserves valuable food but also reduces the environmental footprint associated with production, transportation, and disposal.

One key factor in minimizing losses is the adoption of modern logistics and supply chain management techniques. Temperature-controlled storage and transportation, known as cold chain management, preserves the freshness and quality of perishable foods such as fruits, vegetables, dairy, and meats. Maintaining consistent temperature and humidity levels during transit and storage helps prevent spoilage and reduces the risk of foodborne illness. Innovations such as real-time temperature monitoring and remote sensing enable distributors to quickly detect and respond to any deviations, ensuring that food remains safe and marketable.

Efficient route planning and scheduling are also crucial for reducing distribution losses. By optimizing delivery routes and timing, companies can shorten the time food spends in transit, minimize handling, and avoid unnecessary delays. Technologies like GPS tracking, route optimization software, and predictive analytics support dynamic scheduling and help match supply with demand more accurately. This approach is particularly important for short shelf-life products and in regions with challenging infrastructure.

Collaboration among supply chain partners further reduces losses. Producers, processors, distributors, and retailers can share data on inventory levels, demand forecasts, and delivery timelines to synchronize operations and avoid overstocking or understocking. Transparent communication allows for quick redistribution of surplus or near-expiry products to outlets where they are most needed, reducing waste and supporting food access.

Packaging innovations, such as protective and breathable materials, also help reduce losses by extending shelf life and minimizing damage during transport. Standardizing packaging sizes and shapes streamlines handling, storage, and loading processes, decreasing the risk of spoilage or breakage.

By implementing these strategies, distribution networks become more efficient, resilient, and aligned with circular economy principles. Reducing losses not only supports food security but also unlocks economic and environmental benefits throughout the supply chain.

Sustainable Logistics and Transportation

Sustainable logistics and transportation are key components of a circular food economy, ensuring that food products move efficiently and responsibly from producers to consumers. These functions play a pivotal role in reducing resource consumption, minimizing emissions, and preventing losses and waste along the supply chain.

Transportation accounts for a significant portion of the environmental impact in food systems, with greenhouse gas emissions, energy use, and air pollution resulting from the movement of goods. Shifting to low-carbon transport modes—such as rail, electric vehicles, or vehicles fueled by biogas or renewable energy—helps reduce the carbon footprint of distribution networks. Route optimization technologies and real-time logistics platforms enable companies to plan the shortest and most efficient delivery paths, reducing fuel consumption and improving delivery reliability.

Load optimization further enhances sustainability by ensuring that transport vehicles operate at maximum capacity. Consolidating shipments, using modular or standardized packaging, and coordinating delivery schedules between supply chain partners all contribute to fewer trips and less energy use. Logistics hubs and cross-docking centers facilitate the quick transfer and aggregation of goods, shortening transit times and reducing storage needs.

Cold chain management remains critical for perishable foods. Maintaining consistent temperature and humidity throughout transportation preserves food quality and safety, preventing spoilage and extending shelf life. Advanced monitoring systems and smart sensors track conditions in real time, alerting operators to potential risks and allowing prompt corrective action.

Sustainable logistics also means integrating circular practices, such as the collection and return of reusable packaging or the backhauling of surplus food for redistribution or valorization. Collaboration with suppliers, retailers, and third-party logistics providers fosters innovation and enables the adoption of greener transport options.

Embracing digital technologies, such as IoT, blockchain, and big data analytics, enhances transparency and coordination, supporting more adaptive and resilient supply chains. Data-driven insights inform continuous improvement and enable companies to track their progress toward sustainability targets.

Sustainable logistics and transportation practices reduce environmental impacts, lower operational costs, and support the efficient, reliable delivery of food. These efforts align with the broader goals of circularity and resilience in modern food systems, creating long-term value for businesses, communities, and the environment.

Innovations in Cold Chain and Storage

Innovations in cold chain and storage are transforming how food systems manage perishable goods, directly supporting the goals of a circular food economy. Effective cold chain solutions extend shelf life, reduce food loss and waste, and preserve nutritional quality, ensuring that products reach consumers in optimal condition while minimizing environmental impacts.

Modern cold chain systems incorporate advanced refrigeration technologies that offer greater efficiency and reliability. Variable-speed compressors, natural refrigerants, and energy-efficient insulation materials lower energy consumption and reduce greenhouse gas emissions. Solar-powered refrigeration units are increasingly used in remote or off-grid areas, expanding access to cold storage and enabling small producers to participate in formal markets.

Smart monitoring systems are now standard in many cold storage facilities and transport vehicles. Sensors track temperature, humidity, and other critical conditions in real time, providing immediate alerts when thresholds are breached. Automated data logging and remote access enable operators to respond quickly to deviations, reducing spoilage and loss. This level of control not only ensures food safety but also supports traceability, building trust among supply chain partners and consumers.

Flexible and modular storage solutions have also advanced cold chain logistics. Mobile cold rooms, refrigerated containers, and portable chillers allow for scalable and adaptable storage capacity, accommodating fluctuations in supply and demand or seasonal harvests. Shared cold storage facilities and logistics hubs enable collective use by multiple producers, reducing costs and increasing efficiency for small-scale operations.

Packaging innovations complement cold chain improvements. Breathable, moisture-regulating, and insulating materials protect products during storage and transport, reducing spoilage without relying on excessive plastic or non-recyclable packaging. Integration of active packaging with freshness indicators provides real-time information on product condition, supporting quality control and timely distribution decisions.

Circularity is further enhanced by initiatives that recover and redistribute surplus or near-expiry products from storage facilities, diverting edible food from waste streams and supporting food security programs. Reuse and refurbishment of refrigeration equipment, along with proper disposal and recycling of obsolete units, minimize resource consumption and environmental impacts.

Ongoing investment in innovative cold chain and storage solutions strengthens food system resilience and sustainability. These advancements ensure high-quality food reaches consumers while supporting the transition to more efficient and circular supply chains.

Circular Approaches in Retail Operations

Circular approaches in retail operations are central to reducing waste, promoting resource efficiency, and enabling a sustainable food system. Retailers occupy a unique position in the food value chain, connecting producers to consumers and shaping purchasing behaviors, product offerings, and end-of-life outcomes for food and packaging.

A key strategy involves optimizing inventory management to align supply with actual demand, reducing the risk of surplus stock, spoilage, and markdowns. Advanced forecasting tools, real-time sales analytics, and data sharing with suppliers help retailers respond quickly to shifting consumer preferences and minimize unsold inventory. Dynamic pricing models and targeted promotions for products nearing expiration further reduce the likelihood of waste.

In-store initiatives play an important role in supporting circularity. Bulk dispensing stations and refillable product lines encourage shoppers to purchase only what they need while minimizing single-use packaging. Stores can introduce reusable bag schemes, incentivize the return of containers, or collaborate with suppliers on deposit-refund programs for packaging.

Redistribution of surplus or near-expiry products is another circular strategy. Partnering with food banks, charities, and food rescue organizations ensures that edible products are diverted from landfill and reach those in need. Some retailers also process surplus into ready-to-eat meals or discounted products, adding value and reducing waste simultaneously.

Sustainable design and material selection for private-label packaging further advance circularity. Choosing recyclable, compostable, or reusable packaging materials and providing clear instructions for proper disposal empower consumers to participate in circular practices beyond the store.

Employee training and customer engagement campaigns foster a culture of sustainability throughout retail operations. Staff are equipped to manage waste-reduction initiatives and communicate the benefits of circularity to customers, creating shared responsibility for more sustainable consumption.

Circular retail operations strengthen brand reputation, reduce operational costs, and align with growing consumer demand for sustainable products. Retailers that lead in circularity contribute to broader food system transformation, demonstrating that commerce and sustainability can go hand in hand.

Retailer-Consumer Partnerships for Sustainability

Retailer-consumer partnerships play a pivotal role in advancing sustainability and circularity within food systems. By fostering collaboration, transparency, and shared responsibility, retailers and consumers can co-create solutions that reduce waste, promote resource efficiency, and support the shift toward a more sustainable food economy.

Retailers have the ability to guide consumer choices through thoughtful product selection, store design, and information sharing. Promoting products with sustainable attributes—such as organic, local, seasonal, or minimally packaged goods—empowers consumers to make environmentally responsible decisions. Clear labeling, in-store displays, and digital platforms provide accessible information on sourcing, environmental impact, and proper disposal or reuse, helping consumers align their purchases with their values.

Engagement initiatives such as loyalty programs, incentives for returning reusable containers, or discounts on products near expiration actively involve consumers in circular practices. Campaigns that highlight the benefits of waste reduction, resource recovery, or sustainable packaging encourage shoppers to participate in programs that extend product life cycles and minimize environmental harm. Educational workshops, recipe cards for using leftovers, and tips for proper food storage can further inspire behavior change and reduce household waste.

Partnerships also enable feedback loops between retailers and consumers. Customer input on product design, packaging, and sustainability initiatives helps retailers tailor offerings and innovate new solutions. Retailers can use digital surveys, social media platforms, and customer service channels to gather suggestions and respond to consumer preferences, creating a sense of ownership and collaboration.

The success of circular and sustainable initiatives depends on building trust and mutual benefit. Transparent communication about goals, progress, and challenges helps establish credibility, while shared rewards reinforce positive behaviors. Retailers that engage consumers as active partners in sustainability not only reduce their own environmental footprint but also cultivate loyal customer bases.

Retailer-consumer partnerships strengthen community engagement, drive innovation, and contribute to the broader adoption of circular practices throughout the food system. This collaborative approach accelerates progress toward sustainability goals and demonstrates the power of collective action.

Reducing Food Waste in Supermarkets

Reducing food waste in supermarkets is a crucial element of the circular food economy, as supermarkets are key points where significant volumes of edible food can be lost due to overstocking, improper handling, or consumer demand fluctuations. Tackling this challenge requires a combination of strategic management, technological innovation, and partnerships across the supply chain.

Effective inventory management lies at the heart of waste reduction efforts. Supermarkets increasingly use predictive analytics and real-time data to track sales patterns, anticipate demand, and optimize restocking schedules. This approach minimizes overordering and helps maintain inventory levels that reflect actual consumer needs, reducing the likelihood of products expiring on the shelves.

Smart shelving and digital monitoring systems further support waste reduction. Shelves equipped with sensors can monitor stock levels and expiration dates, triggering automated alerts for timely markdowns or removal of at-risk items. These systems enable staff to prioritize the sale of products that are nearing their best-before date and apply dynamic pricing to encourage quick purchase.

Clear labeling and consumer education also play important roles. Providing transparent information about date labels—distinguishing between "best before" and "use by" dates—helps consumers make informed decisions and prevents premature disposal of safe, edible food. In-store campaigns, signage, and staff training support these efforts and foster a culture of waste reduction.

Redistribution and donation of surplus food offer a direct route to divert edible products from landfill. Partnerships with food banks, charities, and food rescue organizations facilitate the collection and redistribution of unsold but still safe-to-eat goods. Some supermarkets also repurpose surplus produce into prepared foods, juices, or meal kits, creating additional value and reducing waste simultaneously.

Innovative packaging solutions extend shelf life and preserve product quality, while refrigeration and humidity controls help maintain freshness. Supermarkets can also adopt reusable or compostable packaging to address packaging waste in tandem with food waste reduction.

Collaboration with suppliers and producers ensures that ordering practices are flexible and responsive to supply variations, helping to balance the flow of goods and avoid excess stock.

Through these combined strategies, supermarkets not only reduce food waste but also strengthen their reputation, lower operational costs, and contribute to food security in their communities. This holistic approach reinforces the principles of a circular economy and drives progress toward more sustainable food systems.

Policy and Business Models for Circular Retail

Effective policy frameworks and innovative business models are vital for embedding circularity into retail operations and driving systemic change across the food sector. These approaches create the enabling environment and economic incentives necessary for retailers to transition from linear to circular practices, reduce waste, and promote resource efficiency.

Policy support takes several forms. Governments and local authorities may introduce regulations that set targets for food waste reduction, require transparent reporting, or ban the disposal of edible food. Extended producer responsibility (EPR) schemes can make retailers accountable for the packaging and products they place on the market, encouraging the use of recyclable, reusable, or compostable materials. Fiscal incentives, such as tax breaks, grants, or subsidies, lower the financial barriers to adopting circular solutions, from installing food donation infrastructure to developing sustainable packaging.

Public procurement policies that favor retailers with strong circular credentials encourage businesses to implement best practices in waste prevention, surplus redistribution, and sustainable sourcing. Certification schemes and labeling programs, such as zero-waste or circular economy certifications, offer recognition and marketing advantages to retailers who demonstrate leadership in circularity.

On the business model front, circular retail embraces new ways of delivering value to customers while minimizing environmental impact. Refill stations, package-free shopping, and product-as-a-service models allow consumers to access goods without generating unnecessary waste. Deposit-return schemes incentivize customers to return packaging for reuse or recycling, supporting closed-loop systems and reducing single-use plastics.

Retailers may also develop platforms for direct sales of surplus or imperfect products, turning potential waste into new revenue streams. Collaboration with local producers, food rescue organizations, and logistics partners supports the redistribution of unsold goods and the creation of secondary product lines, such as meal kits or upcycled foods.

Digital platforms and data analytics play a crucial role in implementing these models, enabling real-time inventory management, dynamic pricing, and customer engagement. Technology facilitates transparency, compliance, and communication with stakeholders, ensuring that circular practices are effectively embedded in daily operations.

Through a combination of supportive policies and innovative business models, retail operations can move toward circularity, unlocking new opportunities for growth, reducing their environmental footprint, and aligning with consumer demand for sustainable solutions.

Chapter 5: Circular Consumption and Consumer Engagement

Circular consumption and active consumer engagement are central to driving change throughout the food system. This chapter explores how households, communities, and institutions can adopt behaviors and practices that minimize food waste, support sustainable diets, and close resource loops. Key themes include education and awareness, food sharing platforms, behavior change strategies, and the influence of social norms. The chapter also examines the role of policy instruments and community initiatives in making circular options accessible and attractive. Through collective action and informed choices, consumers play a pivotal role in building a sustainable, circular food economy.

Promoting Sustainable Diets and Nutrition

Promoting sustainable diets and nutrition is a cornerstone of the circular food economy, shaping not only what is produced and consumed but also influencing the overall health of people and the planet. Sustainable diets are those that have low environmental impacts, contribute to food and nutrition security, and support healthy lives for present and future generations.

A sustainable diet prioritizes diversity, seasonality, and the inclusion of more plant-based foods, such as fruits, vegetables, legumes, whole grains, nuts, and seeds. These foods require fewer resources—land, water, and energy—to produce compared to animal-based products and typically have a lower carbon footprint. Incorporating moderate amounts of sustainably produced animal-source foods can further support balanced nutrition while reducing the pressure on ecosystems.

Education and public awareness campaigns are powerful tools for encouraging shifts toward more sustainable eating patterns. Governments, health agencies, and retailers can provide clear, evidence-based guidance on healthy, environmentally friendly food choices through dietary guidelines, food labeling, and in-store promotions. Initiatives such as "meatless days," plant-forward menus, or local food festivals inspire consumers to explore and embrace diverse, sustainable foods.

Nutrition-sensitive food policies and social protection programs play a key role in making sustainable diets accessible and affordable for all. Support for local farmers' markets, community-supported agriculture, and urban gardening initiatives strengthens local food systems and connects consumers to fresh, seasonal, and minimally processed foods. Subsidies and incentives for fruits, vegetables, and whole grains make healthy options more economically attractive.

Food industry actors—including manufacturers, retailers, and food service providers—also influence dietary habits by reformulating products, reducing portion sizes, and expanding the range of nutritious, sustainable offerings. Transparent communication about sourcing, environmental impacts, and nutritional value empowers consumers to make informed decisions.

Cultural preferences, traditions, and taste must be respected in the transition to sustainable diets. Successful strategies honor local food cultures while introducing healthier, more sustainable choices in ways that are appealing and accessible.

Widespread adoption of sustainable diets supports individual well-being, reduces pressure on natural resources, and lowers greenhouse gas emissions. These positive impacts reinforce the foundations of a circular food economy, creating synergies between health, sustainability, and food system resilience.

Behavior Change for Waste Reduction

Behavior change is a critical driver in reducing food waste and advancing the goals of a circular food economy. The daily habits and choices of individuals, households, and organizations collectively determine how much food is purchased, prepared, consumed, and ultimately wasted. Promoting sustainable behaviors at every level of society helps minimize waste and ensures that resources are used efficiently.

Awareness and education form the foundation for effective behavior change. Public campaigns, community workshops, and school programs raise awareness about the environmental, economic, and social impacts of food waste. Simple, practical tips—such as meal planning, proper storage techniques, and understanding date labels—empower consumers to shop more mindfully and use food before it spoils. Visual reminders in kitchens or stores and accessible digital tools, like food tracking apps and recipe finders, encourage people to make the most of what they have.

In households, behavior change often begins with meal planning and shopping lists. Planning meals in advance, buying only what is needed, and using leftovers for future meals significantly reduce the amount of food that ends up in the bin. Proper storage—refrigerating perishable items, using airtight containers, and rotating older items to the front of the fridge or pantry—helps maintain freshness and prevents spoilage.

Portion control and mindful eating also contribute to waste reduction. Preparing and serving appropriate portion sizes minimizes plate waste, while sharing excess food with friends, neighbors, or through food-sharing platforms ensures that surplus is used rather than discarded. Cooking creatively with leftovers or ingredients close to expiry extends the usefulness of food and adds variety to meals.

Institutions and businesses play an important role in shaping food waste behaviors. Restaurants, cafeterias, and supermarkets can offer smaller portion options, highlight "ugly" but edible produce, and donate surplus food to local charities. Clear communication and positive reinforcement encourage staff and customers to participate in waste-reduction initiatives.

Long-term behavior change requires supportive policies, community engagement, and convenient solutions that make sustainable choices easy and rewarding. Recognizing and celebrating positive actions—through incentives, public recognition, or community challenges—reinforces habits and builds a culture of resourcefulness.

Through sustained behavior change at every level, food waste can be dramatically reduced, supporting a more efficient, resilient, and circular food system.

Role of Education and Public Awareness

Education and public awareness are foundational elements in promoting circularity within food systems and achieving lasting change in consumption and waste patterns. Equipping individuals, households, and organizations with knowledge about food's journey—from production to disposal—empowers them to make informed, sustainable choices that support the goals of a circular food economy.

Integrating food system education into school curricula establishes sustainable habits from an early age. Lessons on nutrition, environmental impacts, and responsible consumption foster understanding of how daily choices affect both personal health and planetary well-being. School gardens, composting projects, and hands-on cooking classes provide practical experiences that connect students to food origins and the value of minimizing waste.

For adults and communities, public awareness campaigns play a vital role. Media initiatives, community workshops, and digital resources spread key messages about the consequences of food waste, the benefits of sustainable diets, and the importance of resource recovery. Effective campaigns use clear, relatable messaging—such as tips for meal planning, creative use of leftovers, and guidance on understanding food labeling—to inspire action at home and in the workplace.

Retailers, food producers, and hospitality businesses contribute to education by offering information at points of purchase and consumption. In-store signage, digital displays, and product labeling provide shoppers with details on environmental impacts, sourcing, storage, and end-of-life options. Restaurants and cafeterias can highlight sustainable menu choices, explain portion sizes, and share stories about local sourcing or surplus redistribution efforts.

Social media platforms amplify educational efforts, connecting consumers with real-time updates, inspiring stories, and practical tools. Influencers, chefs, and community leaders can model positive behaviors and demonstrate easy steps for reducing waste and embracing circular practices.

Collaboration among government agencies, non-profits, businesses, and educators is essential for reaching diverse audiences and ensuring consistent messaging. Programs that recognize and celebrate waste reduction achievements—such as awards, certifications, or public challenges—motivate participation and build a culture of sustainability.

When education and awareness become widespread and accessible, they transform knowledge into action. Informed communities are better equipped to make choices that reduce waste, support sustainable food systems, and drive the transition toward a circular economy.

Food Sharing and Redistribution Platforms

Food sharing and redistribution platforms are instrumental in reducing food waste and promoting circularity within food systems. These platforms connect sources of surplus food—such as supermarkets, restaurants, producers, and households—with individuals and organizations that can make use of edible items that might otherwise be discarded.

Digital platforms and mobile apps have transformed how surplus food is shared or redistributed. Users can quickly list, claim, and collect available food in their local area, making the redistribution process efficient and accessible. Community fridges, food-sharing hubs, and local exchange programs enable residents to donate or collect surplus items, strengthening neighborhood ties and supporting food security.

Retailers and food service businesses often partner with charitable organizations, food banks, and social enterprises to streamline the donation of surplus products. These partnerships are supported by logistics solutions that ensure safe and timely transport, as well as quality assurance measures to maintain food safety standards. Food rescue organizations coordinate the collection and distribution of surplus from multiple sources, efficiently delivering food to those in need while reducing the burden on landfills.

Technology-driven solutions play a critical role in scaling food redistribution. Platforms equipped with real-time inventory management, automated notifications, and data analytics help match supply and demand, identify trends, and optimize operations. Transparency features—such as donation tracking and impact reporting—build trust and encourage ongoing participation among donors and recipients.

Household-level food sharing is also gaining popularity, with apps and social networks allowing individuals to exchange extra meals, ingredients, or garden produce with neighbors. These initiatives foster community engagement, reduce waste, and provide access to fresh food.

Food sharing and redistribution platforms not only prevent edible food from going to waste but also contribute to broader social and environmental goals. By supporting community networks, improving food access, and reducing the environmental impacts of waste disposal, these platforms exemplify the practical benefits of circularity in action.

Engaging Households in Circular Practices

Engaging households in circular practices is fundamental to creating a resilient and sustainable food system. The decisions made in home kitchens—including how food is purchased, stored, prepared, and disposed of—have a significant impact on resource efficiency and waste generation throughout the food value chain.

Households can begin adopting circular practices by rethinking how food is sourced and consumed. Choosing locally produced, seasonal, and minimally packaged foods reduces the environmental footprint of daily meals. Participating in community-supported agriculture, farmers' markets, or food cooperatives fosters connections with local producers and encourages more mindful consumption.

Meal planning and smart shopping are central to minimizing food waste at home. By making grocery lists, purchasing only what is needed, and considering meal portions, households avoid unnecessary purchases and reduce the likelihood of spoilage. Regularly checking pantry and fridge inventories helps ensure that older items are used first, preventing them from being forgotten and thrown away.

Proper storage extends the shelf life of fresh foods. Using airtight containers, adjusting fridge temperatures, and storing produce in the correct environment—such as cool, dark spaces for root vegetables or breathable bags for leafy greens—maintain freshness and quality. Labeling leftovers with dates and rotating them to the front of the fridge makes it easier to use them promptly.

Creative cooking and reuse of ingredients further support circularity. Repurposing leftovers into new meals, transforming vegetable trimmings into broths, and using overripe fruit for baking or smoothies all maximize the value of food and minimize waste. Sharing surplus meals with neighbors or through community food-sharing initiatives extends the benefits of circular practices beyond the household.

Household composting transforms unavoidable food scraps into valuable soil amendments, closing nutrient loops and supporting home or community gardens. Access to local composting facilities or municipal organic waste collection makes it easier for households to participate in resource recovery.

Education and awareness programs tailored for households—such as workshops, online resources, and social media campaigns—provide practical tips, recipes, and inspiration for adopting circular habits. Incentives, such as discounts for using reusable packaging or rewards for participating in food waste reduction programs, further encourage engagement.

When households embrace circular practices, they help drive systemic change across the food system, reducing waste, conserving resources, and supporting local economies. Collective household action amplifies the impact of circularity, making sustainable food systems a shared reality.

The Influence of Social Norms and Communities

Social norms and community dynamics have a powerful influence on the adoption of circular practices within food systems. The behaviors, attitudes, and expectations shared among members of a community often shape individual decisions, either reinforcing traditional patterns of consumption and waste or encouraging more sustainable habits.

When sustainable practices such as meal planning, composting, or food sharing become visible and normalized within a community, individuals are more likely to emulate these behaviors. Social acceptance of practices like bringing reusable bags, shopping at local markets, or participating in community composting signals to others that these actions are valued and desirable. Community leaders, influencers, and early adopters play an important role in modeling these behaviors and inspiring broader participation.

Public recognition and celebration of waste reduction achievements further reinforce positive social norms. Community events, challenges, or awards programs that highlight individuals and groups making progress in circularity create a sense of pride and shared purpose. Storytelling and local media coverage can amplify these successes, spreading awareness and motivating others to get involved.

Social networks also facilitate the exchange of resources, information, and support. Neighborhood groups, online forums, and community organizations provide platforms for sharing surplus food, swapping recipes, or organizing group purchases of sustainable goods. These interactions build trust, strengthen relationships, and make it easier for individuals to try new practices.

Communities that foster collaboration and inclusivity tend to be more effective in driving lasting behavior change. Engaging diverse groups—across ages, cultures, and socioeconomic backgrounds—ensures that circular initiatives are accessible and relevant to all members. Collaborative projects such as community gardens, food co-ops, or repair cafes create tangible opportunities for learning and involvement.

The collective impact of social norms and community engagement accelerates the adoption of circular practices. As sustainable behaviors become the standard within a community, they help shift broader cultural expectations, supporting the long-term transition to resilient and circular food systems.

Policy Instruments to Support Circular Consumption

Policy instruments are crucial tools for steering consumer behavior and supporting the widespread adoption of circular practices in food systems. Through a mix of regulatory measures, economic incentives, and educational initiatives, policymakers can create enabling environments that make sustainable and circular choices accessible, appealing, and rewarding for individuals and households.

Regulatory instruments set clear rules and standards for sustainable consumption. These may include bans or restrictions on single-use plastics, requirements for recyclable or compostable packaging, and mandates for transparent food labeling to help consumers make informed choices. Minimum durability standards for food-related products, such as reusable containers or utensils, encourage longer use cycles and reduce the generation of waste.

Economic incentives play a powerful role in changing behavior. Subsidies, tax reductions, or rebates for the purchase of sustainable products—such as home composting kits, reusable packaging, or energy-efficient appliances—lower financial barriers and encourage adoption. Conversely, environmental taxes or levies on products that generate excessive waste, such as disposable cutlery or overpackaged goods, discourage unsustainable consumption.

EPR schemes are another important instrument. EPR policies require manufacturers and retailers to take responsibility for the end-of-life management of the products and packaging they introduce to the market. This not only drives improvements in product design but also supports the development of return, refill, and recycling systems that make circular consumption more convenient for consumers.

Information-based instruments complement regulatory and economic measures by increasing awareness and empowering choice. Government campaigns, labeling programs, and certification schemes highlight the benefits of circular practices and help consumers identify products and services that align with sustainability goals. Public recognition, awards, and challenges reward households and communities that demonstrate leadership in waste reduction and circularity.

Policies that promote access to food-sharing networks, surplus redistribution programs, and community composting make it easier for consumers to participate in resource recovery and waste prevention. Local governments can support infrastructure and services that facilitate circular behaviors, such as drop-off points for reusable packaging or public composting sites.

The strategic use of policy instruments creates a supportive ecosystem where circular consumption can flourish. Well-designed policies remove barriers, provide positive incentives, and embed circularity into daily life, accelerating the transition toward sustainable, resilient food systems.

Chapter 6: Food Waste Prevention and Valorization

Preventing and valorizing food waste are at the heart of the circular food economy, turning potential losses into valuable resources for society and the environment. This chapter examines the scale and causes of food waste across the food chain and presents strategies for prevention at every stage—from production and processing to retail and the home. It also explores innovative approaches for recovering value from unavoidable waste, such as bioenergy, compost, and high-value bioproducts. By adopting these practices, food systems can reduce their environmental impact, enhance resource efficiency, and support sustainability goals.

Understanding the Scale and Impact of Food Waste

Food waste is a global challenge with significant environmental, economic, and social consequences. Each year, a substantial portion of food produced for human consumption is lost or wasted along the supply chain—from farms and processing facilities to retailers and households. This inefficiency undermines food security, squanders natural resources, and contributes to climate change.

Globally, it is estimated that nearly one-third of all food produced is lost or wasted. These losses occur at different stages, depending on the context. In low-income regions, much of the waste happens during harvesting, storage, and transport due to inadequate infrastructure, lack of technology, or insufficient market access. In higher-income countries, food waste is most pronounced at the retail and consumer levels, often resulting from over-purchasing, strict cosmetic standards, confusion over date labeling, and cultural attitudes toward abundance.

The environmental impact of food waste is profound. When food is wasted, so too are the land, water, energy, and labor that went into its production. Food that ends up in landfills decomposes anaerobically, generating methane, a potent greenhouse gas. The unnecessary use of resources and subsequent emissions contribute to biodiversity loss, water scarcity, and climate change, intensifying pressure on already fragile ecosystems.

Food waste also carries significant economic costs. Producers, processors, retailers, and consumers all incur losses from food that is grown, processed, and transported but never consumed. At the household level, food waste represents wasted spending, while businesses lose potential revenue and may incur disposal fees. Reducing food waste presents an opportunity for cost savings and efficiency improvements across the food system.

On the social front, food waste coexists with persistent hunger and malnutrition in many regions. Redirecting surplus edible food to those in need through food rescue and redistribution programs can help address food insecurity while reducing waste.

Understanding the scale and impact of food waste is essential for designing effective solutions. Data collection, measurement, and transparent reporting at every stage of the supply chain inform targeted strategies and track progress. Raising awareness among all stakeholders supports collective action, making food waste reduction a shared priority for building more sustainable, circular food systems.

Prevention Strategies Across the Food Chain

Preventing food waste requires a comprehensive approach that addresses inefficiencies and losses at every stage of the food chain— from production and processing to distribution, retail, and consumption. By targeting the root causes of waste, prevention strategies maximize the value of resources, strengthen food security, and support the transition to a circular food economy.

At the production level, prevention begins with improved planning and management. Farmers can use forecasting tools, market information, and precision agriculture technologies to better match crop production to demand, minimizing surplus harvests. Selecting resilient crop varieties, optimizing planting schedules, and investing in improved storage and transport infrastructure help reduce losses caused by weather, pests, or spoilage.

During processing and manufacturing, maximizing raw material use and improving quality control are key strategies. Facilities can implement automated sorting and grading systems to make the most of every batch, repurposing by-products into new products, animal feed, or compost instead of sending them to landfill. Adopting lean manufacturing principles and monitoring equipment for efficiency further reduces waste.

Distribution and logistics play a critical role in prevention. Efficient supply chain management—such as temperature control, real-time tracking, and demand-driven logistics—preserves the quality and freshness of food in transit. Collaboration among supply chain partners, data sharing, and flexible ordering systems enable better alignment between supply and demand, reducing the risk of unsold or expired products.

Retailers can adopt strategies such as dynamic pricing, product markdowns, and consumer education to encourage the sale of items approaching their best-before date. Clear labeling, smaller portion packaging, and promotion of "imperfect" but edible produce also help prevent food from being discarded unnecessarily.

At the consumer level, raising awareness and providing practical guidance on meal planning, storage, and portion sizes empower households to minimize waste. Food sharing platforms and community initiatives make it easier for surplus food to be redistributed or repurposed, closing the loop and preventing avoidable losses.

Prevention is always the most effective strategy for tackling food waste. By integrating solutions at every stage and fostering collaboration among all stakeholders, food systems can conserve resources, lower costs, and contribute to environmental and social sustainability. Prevention not only reduces waste but also builds resilience and circularity into the heart of the food economy.

Surplus Food Recovery and Redistribution

Surplus food recovery and redistribution are central strategies in circular food systems, ensuring that edible food, which might otherwise be wasted, reaches those who can benefit from it. These practices reduce the environmental and economic impacts of food waste, support food security, and build stronger community networks.

Surplus food arises at multiple points along the supply chain—from farms and food processors to retailers, restaurants, and households. Common causes include overproduction, cosmetic imperfections, changes in demand, or approaching expiration dates. While some surplus food is unavoidable, well-designed recovery and redistribution systems ensure it is put to the best possible use.

The first step in surplus food recovery is identifying and collecting edible products that are safe for consumption but unsuitable for sale. Technology platforms and digital inventory systems play a significant role in tracking surplus and matching it with organizations or individuals in need. Businesses can partner with food banks, charities, and food rescue organizations to coordinate efficient pick-up, storage, and distribution of surplus goods.

Cold chain logistics and proper handling procedures are essential for maintaining the safety and quality of recovered food, especially for perishable items. Investments in transport, storage, and volunteer networks help ensure that food is delivered quickly and safely to recipients.

Redistribution models vary widely, from large-scale operations supplying schools, shelters, and community kitchens to grassroots efforts like community fridges and local food sharing platforms. In addition to supporting vulnerable populations, these initiatives foster social inclusion and community engagement.

Legal frameworks and liability protections, such as Good Samaritan laws, encourage businesses to donate surplus food without fear of litigation. Policy incentives, including tax deductions or grants for food donation infrastructure, further support widespread participation.

Education and awareness campaigns highlight the benefits of surplus food recovery, breaking down stigma and building trust among donors, recipients, and the public. Transparent reporting and impact tracking help measure progress, demonstrate value, and inspire ongoing involvement.

Recovering and redistributing surplus food diverts resources from waste streams, reduces greenhouse gas emissions, and helps meet the needs of food-insecure populations. Through collaborative action and innovative models, surplus food recovery becomes a pillar of circularity and sustainability in modern food systems.

Valorizing Food Waste: Bioenergy and Bioproducts

Valorizing food waste through the production of bioenergy and bioproducts transforms a traditional liability into valuable resources, supporting the circular food economy and reducing environmental impacts. Rather than sending food waste to landfill, innovative technologies recover energy, nutrients, and materials, closing resource loops and creating new economic opportunities.

Bioenergy generation is a key pathway for food waste valorization. Anaerobic digestion is widely used to break down organic matter— such as food scraps, processing residues, and manure—under oxygen-free conditions. This process produces biogas, a renewable energy source that can be used for electricity, heating, or vehicle fuel. The remaining digestate is nutrient-rich and serves as a high-quality organic fertilizer, returning valuable nutrients to agricultural soils and reducing the need for synthetic alternatives.

Composting is another effective method for converting food waste into useful products. By managing the decomposition process under controlled aerobic conditions, composting transforms organic waste into humus-like material that enhances soil fertility, improves structure, and increases water retention. Community-scale and municipal composting programs make it possible for households and businesses to participate in nutrient recovery and waste reduction.

Beyond energy and fertilizers, emerging technologies are unlocking new value streams from food waste. Fermentation, enzymatic treatment, and extraction processes can isolate proteins, fibers, and bioactive compounds from waste materials. These ingredients find use in animal feed, bioplastics, packaging materials, pharmaceuticals, and even cosmetics. For example, food industry by-products can be processed into biodegradable packaging, reducing reliance on fossil-based plastics and supporting closed-loop material cycles.

Integrated biorefineries represent a holistic approach to valorizing food waste, using multiple technologies to recover energy, chemicals, and materials from a single waste stream. This model supports the efficient use of resources, maximizes value, and reduces environmental burdens associated with disposal.

Policy frameworks and investment in research and infrastructure are essential to scale up food waste valorization. Regulations that incentivize resource recovery and support innovation help bring new solutions to market and expand participation across sectors.

Valorizing food waste through bioenergy and bioproducts not only mitigates environmental harm but also drives economic growth and resilience. These practices are foundational to a circular food system, transforming waste into a source of value and sustainability.

Circular Models in Hospitality and Food Services

Circular models in hospitality and food services are reshaping how food is sourced, prepared, served, and disposed of, placing a strong emphasis on resource efficiency, waste minimization, and environmental stewardship. Restaurants, hotels, catering companies, and institutional kitchens are uniquely positioned to drive change due to their direct influence on food procurement, menu design, and customer engagement.

Sustainable sourcing is a fundamental aspect of circularity in hospitality. By prioritizing local, seasonal, and responsibly produced ingredients, food service providers reduce transport emissions, support regional economies, and promote biodiversity. Establishing supplier partnerships that embrace circular practices—such as reusable packaging, shared delivery systems, or return schemes—further strengthens sustainability across the supply chain.

Menu planning and portion control also play critical roles. Designing flexible menus that use the whole ingredient and feature daily specials based on surplus or seasonal produce helps minimize food waste. Offering varied portion sizes allows customers to choose amounts that fit their needs, reducing plate waste and increasing customer satisfaction.

Kitchen operations incorporate waste-reduction strategies such as proper storage, inventory rotation, and the creative use of trimmings or leftovers in new dishes. Food that is still safe but unsold can be redistributed through partnerships with food rescue organizations, staff meals, or community programs, ensuring it is put to good use.

Reusable and compostable serviceware, as well as the elimination of single-use plastics, are standard practices in circular hospitality models. On-site composting or participation in local organic waste collection closes nutrient loops and provides valuable material for landscaping or gardening.

Education and engagement are essential, with staff trained in sustainable practices and customers encouraged to participate through information, incentives, or feedback opportunities.

Through the adoption of circular models, hospitality and food service businesses reduce their environmental footprint, cut costs, and enhance their reputation. These efforts create a ripple effect, influencing suppliers, partners, and consumers, and contributing to the larger transformation toward circularity in the food sector.

Household Food Waste: Challenges and Solutions

Household food waste presents a persistent challenge in many societies, significantly contributing to the overall loss of resources within food systems. The reasons for waste at the household level are varied and complex, often involving a mix of behavioral, practical, and cultural factors that influence purchasing, storage, preparation, and disposal habits.

A common challenge is the tendency to over-purchase or buy in bulk, driven by promotional offers, convenience, or an aspiration to be well-prepared. Without careful planning, this often leads to forgotten or spoiled food. Confusion over date labels—mistaking "best before" for "use by," or discarding food that is still safe—results in unnecessary disposal. Poor storage practices, such as incorrect refrigeration or neglecting to rotate pantry items, accelerate spoilage and increase waste.

Preparation and portioning habits also play a role. Preparing large meals without considering actual consumption, serving oversized portions, or failing to use leftovers can quickly accumulate waste. Busy lifestyles may prompt households to opt for takeaways or pre-prepared meals, leaving fresh ingredients unused.

To address these challenges, a range of practical solutions can be adopted at the household level. Meal planning and shopping lists help ensure that only necessary items are purchased, reducing surplus and preventing impulse buys. Learning to interpret date labels correctly and applying "first in, first out" rotation in storage minimizes spoilage and extends food usability.

Proper storage is critical for maintaining freshness. Adjusting refrigerator settings, using airtight containers, and organizing shelves to keep older items visible help households make the most of what they have. Creative use of leftovers—transforming them into new meals, snacks, or freezer portions—reduces waste and adds variety to diets.

Education and awareness campaigns tailored for households provide valuable tips, recipes, and motivation for waste reduction. Community initiatives such as food-sharing platforms, local composting programs, and neighborhood swaps extend the impact of household efforts.

Households that adopt these strategies play a direct role in reducing food waste, conserving resources, and supporting circular food systems. Collective action at home contributes to more sustainable consumption and the overall resilience of food economies.

Role of Technology in Food Waste Management

Technology is playing an increasingly pivotal role in managing and reducing food waste across the entire food system, from production and processing to retail and the household. By enabling better measurement, monitoring, and intervention, technology helps address the root causes of waste, unlocks efficiencies, and supports the transition toward a circular food economy.

At the production and processing stages, digital tools and smart sensors provide real-time data on inventory levels, shelf life, and storage conditions. Automated systems detect early signs of spoilage or inefficiency, allowing for swift action to prevent losses. Predictive analytics use historical and current data to forecast demand, optimize harvest times, and align production with market needs, reducing the risk of overproduction and unsold surplus.

In retail, technologies such as electronic shelf labels, dynamic pricing systems, and inventory management software make it easier to track products nearing expiration. These systems can trigger targeted promotions, markdowns, or donations to ensure that edible food is used rather than discarded. Automated stock rotation and replenishment algorithms further minimize waste by maintaining optimal inventory levels.

Mobile apps and digital platforms connect households, businesses, and communities to food-sharing networks, surplus redistribution programs, and donation opportunities. These platforms make it simple for individuals and organizations to offer or claim surplus food, facilitating the efficient movement of edible items to where they are needed most. Smart kitchen appliances and apps help consumers manage shopping lists, monitor expiration dates, and find recipes for using up available ingredients.

Waste tracking and analytics tools support food service providers and hospitality businesses in identifying where and how much waste occurs in their operations. Detailed reporting pinpoints areas for improvement, informs staff training, and measures progress over time.

Emerging technologies such as artificial intelligence and blockchain bring transparency and traceability to food waste management. These systems enable secure data sharing and collaboration across the supply chain, ensuring accountability and building trust among stakeholders.

Investment in technology and innovation not only drives reductions in food waste but also supports compliance with regulations, reduces costs, and creates new business opportunities. As adoption grows, technology will remain an essential enabler of efficient, circular, and sustainable food systems for the future.

Chapter 7: Resource Recovery and Closing the Loop

Resource recovery and closing the loop are fundamental to the circular food economy, ensuring that valuable materials, nutrients, and energy are continually cycled back into food systems. This chapter explores the technologies, policies, and collaborative efforts driving the recovery of water, nutrients, and other resources from food and organic waste. It examines innovations in composting, anaerobic digestion, and advanced recycling, as well as the enabling policies that make resource recovery scalable. By closing the loop, food systems become more regenerative, resilient, and capable of supporting sustainable growth for communities and the environment.

Circular Pathways for Nutrient Recovery

Circular pathways for nutrient recovery are essential for closing the loop in food systems, transforming waste streams into valuable resources that support soil fertility, crop growth, and environmental health. Rather than allowing nutrients from food and organic waste to be lost through disposal, circular food economies recover and recycle these elements, reducing reliance on synthetic fertilizers and minimizing pollution.

Composting is a widely used method for nutrient recovery, converting food scraps, yard waste, and agricultural residues into nutrient-rich compost. This organic amendment improves soil structure, increases water retention, and provides a slow-release source of essential nutrients for plants. Both household-scale and municipal composting programs make it possible to divert significant quantities of organic waste from landfills while enhancing the productivity of urban and rural soils.

Anaerobic digestion is another important pathway, using microorganisms to break down organic materials in the absence of oxygen. This process produces biogas for renewable energy and leaves behind digestate, a nutrient-dense by-product that can be applied directly to fields as fertilizer. Digestate contains nitrogen, phosphorus, potassium, and micronutrients, making it an effective substitute for chemical inputs.

Biochar, created through the pyrolysis of organic matter such as crop residues or food waste, offers a further route for nutrient recovery. When incorporated into soils, biochar improves nutrient retention, enhances microbial activity, and sequesters carbon, contributing to both soil health and climate mitigation.

The recovery of nutrients is also possible from wastewater generated by food processing or household activities. Advanced treatment technologies extract phosphorus, nitrogen, and other elements from wastewater streams, which can then be recycled as fertilizers or soil conditioners. This approach prevents nutrient runoff into waterways, reducing the risk of water pollution and eutrophication.

Circular nutrient recovery is supported by policies and infrastructure that enable separate collection of organic waste, investment in processing facilities, and quality standards for recovered products. Collaboration among municipalities, businesses, farmers, and households ensures that nutrient-rich outputs are returned to productive use.

By embracing circular pathways for nutrient recovery, food systems can close resource loops, reduce environmental impacts, and build resilience in agriculture. This approach underpins a regenerative, circular food economy that sustains productivity while restoring the health of soils and ecosystems.

Composting and Organic Recycling

Composting and organic recycling are foundational practices in the circular food economy, transforming organic waste into valuable resources that support soil health, nutrient cycling, and waste reduction. These processes divert food scraps, yard trimmings, and other biodegradable materials from landfills, reducing greenhouse gas emissions and closing resource loops.

Composting is a natural, biological process in which microorganisms break down organic matter under controlled conditions to produce a stable, nutrient-rich product called compost. This material is a powerful soil amendment, improving soil structure, moisture retention, and aeration while supplying essential nutrients for plant growth. Home composting allows households to manage their own food and garden waste, while community- and municipal-scale operations process larger volumes from neighborhoods, institutions, and businesses.

Effective composting requires a balanced mix of "green" materials (such as fruit and vegetable scraps or grass clippings) and "brown" materials (such as dry leaves or cardboard), along with proper aeration and moisture. Turning piles and monitoring temperature ensure that compost matures evenly and safely, minimizing odors and pathogens.

Organic recycling extends beyond traditional composting to include other processes that recover value from biodegradable materials. Anaerobic digestion, for example, breaks down organic waste in oxygen-free environments, producing biogas for energy and digestate for use as fertilizer. Vermicomposting uses worms to convert food scraps into high-quality castings, which are particularly rich in nutrients and beneficial microbes.

Municipal organic recycling programs enable widespread participation by providing curbside collection, drop-off centers, or neighborhood composting sites. These programs typically accept food scraps, yard trimmings, and sometimes even compostable packaging, diverting large volumes from landfill disposal. Finished compost is often made available for public landscaping, urban agriculture, or private gardens, completing the resource loop.

Public education is key to successful composting and organic recycling. Clear guidelines on what can and cannot be composted, along with information on the benefits of organic recycling, encourage participation and proper sorting.

Expanding access to composting and organic recycling supports waste reduction, soil regeneration, and climate action. These practices create value from materials once considered waste, advancing the goals of a resilient and regenerative food system.

Anaerobic Digestion and Biogas Production

Anaerobic digestion and biogas production are vital technologies in the circular food economy, enabling the transformation of organic waste into renewable energy and valuable by-products. This process not only diverts food and agricultural waste from landfills but also supports nutrient recycling, emissions reduction, and sustainable resource management.

Anaerobic digestion is a biological process in which microorganisms break down organic matter—such as food scraps, livestock manure, and food processing residues—in the absence of oxygen. The process takes place in sealed, oxygen-free reactors called digesters. As the organic material decomposes, it produces biogas—a mixture primarily composed of methane and carbon dioxide—that can be captured and used as a source of renewable energy. Biogas can generate electricity, provide heat for industrial processes or buildings, or be upgraded and injected into natural gas grids for use as vehicle fuel.

A key by-product of anaerobic digestion is digestate, a nutrient-rich substance that remains after the digestion process is complete. Digestate contains valuable plant nutrients, including nitrogen, phosphorus, and potassium, and can be applied directly to agricultural land as a biofertilizer. This closes nutrient loops, reduces reliance on synthetic fertilizers, and returns organic matter to soils, enhancing their structure and fertility.

Anaerobic digestion offers several environmental benefits. By diverting organic waste from landfills, it prevents the release of methane—a potent greenhouse gas—produced by uncontrolled decomposition. The use of biogas as an energy source offsets fossil fuel consumption, further reducing carbon emissions. Digesters can also be integrated into wastewater treatment plants, improving energy efficiency and enabling nutrient recovery from municipal waste streams.

Successful anaerobic digestion projects rely on careful feedstock management, appropriate reactor design, and regular monitoring to ensure optimal performance. Investment in infrastructure, supportive policy frameworks, and collaboration among waste producers, energy utilities, and farmers are essential for scaling up biogas production.

Education and outreach help raise awareness of the benefits of anaerobic digestion and encourage participation from households, businesses, and communities. Expanding the use of this technology advances the circular food economy by turning waste into energy and biofertilizer, supporting sustainability, and building more resilient food and resource systems.

Circular Water Management in Food Systems

Circular water management in food systems is a crucial element of sustainability, focusing on the efficient use, recovery, and reuse of water resources throughout the food value chain. As agriculture and food processing are among the largest consumers of freshwater globally, implementing circular approaches to water management helps conserve limited supplies, reduce pollution, and build resilience against water scarcity.

At the production level, circular water management begins with precision irrigation technologies, such as drip irrigation and soil moisture sensors, which deliver water directly to plant roots in the optimal amounts. Rainwater harvesting systems capture and store precipitation for later use, reducing dependence on surface and groundwater sources. Reusing treated agricultural runoff or greywater for irrigation supports resource conservation and prevents nutrient-laden water from entering rivers and lakes.

In food processing facilities, water is used for cleaning, cooling, and transporting products. Closed-loop water systems treat and recycle process water, allowing it to be reused multiple times within the facility. Technologies like membrane filtration and ultraviolet disinfection ensure that recycled water meets safety and quality standards. This reduces both the demand for freshwater and the volume of wastewater discharged into the environment.

Nutrient recovery from wastewater further supports circularity. By capturing and reusing nutrients found in process water, facilities can create organic fertilizers and minimize the loss of valuable resources. Advanced treatment systems can also remove contaminants, making the recovered water safe for non-potable uses such as irrigation, equipment cleaning, or cooling.

Adopting circular water management practices requires investment in infrastructure, training, and monitoring. Collaboration between farmers, processors, technology providers, and regulators is essential for developing integrated solutions that are both effective and scalable.

Circular approaches to water management not only conserve a critical resource but also lower operational costs and reduce environmental impacts. These strategies help food systems adapt to the growing pressures of climate change, population growth, and shifting water availability, ensuring long-term sustainability and resilience.

Innovations in Resource Recovery Technologies

Innovations in resource recovery technologies are driving the transformation of food systems toward circularity, enabling the extraction of valuable materials, energy, and nutrients from what was once considered waste. These advancements help close resource loops, reduce environmental impacts, and create new economic opportunities for producers, processors, and communities.

One major area of innovation is the development of advanced separation and extraction technologies. Membrane filtration, centrifugation, and supercritical fluid extraction allow for the efficient recovery of proteins, oils, fibers, and micronutrients from food processing by-products. These recovered components can be used in food manufacturing, animal feed, pharmaceuticals, or biodegradable packaging, turning waste streams into sources of value.

Biotechnological solutions are also expanding the possibilities for resource recovery. Enzyme-assisted extraction and microbial fermentation can convert agricultural residues, food waste, and side streams into a variety of products, such as bio-based chemicals, bioplastics, organic acids, and specialty ingredients. These processes are designed to maximize yield and minimize residual waste, supporting the overall goal of circularity.

Resource recovery is advancing in the field of energy as well. Anaerobic digestion and pyrolysis technologies produce renewable energy in the form of biogas or bio-oil, while also generating nutrient-rich by-products like digestate or biochar for use in agriculture. Innovations in process integration allow food producers and processors to generate power, heat, and valuable soil amendments from their own waste streams, reducing costs and environmental burdens.

Water recycling and nutrient recovery technologies are increasingly integrated into processing facilities. Systems that capture, treat, and purify wastewater allow for its reuse in cleaning, cooling, or irrigation, while nutrient extraction technologies recover phosphorus, nitrogen, and potassium for use as fertilizers. These approaches prevent resource loss and reduce pollution, supporting sustainable water and nutrient management.

Digital technologies play a crucial role in optimizing resource recovery operations. Real-time monitoring, data analytics, and automated control systems enable precise management of recovery processes, ensuring efficiency and quality.

Investment in research, supportive policy frameworks, and cross-sector collaboration are accelerating the adoption of these innovative technologies. As resource recovery solutions become more sophisticated and widely accessible, food systems move closer to achieving true circularity, resilience, and sustainability.

Enabling Policies for Resource Recovery

Enabling policies are fundamental to scaling up resource recovery in food systems, creating the incentives, standards, and support structures needed to transform waste into valuable resources. Policymakers play a crucial role in shaping the regulatory environment, removing barriers, and fostering innovation across the food value chain.

Regulatory frameworks that prioritize waste prevention and resource recovery set clear expectations for all stakeholders. Mandates for source separation of organic waste, landfill bans for biodegradable materials, and requirements for recycling or composting encourage businesses and households to divert waste from disposal and participate in recovery initiatives. Environmental standards for compost quality, digestate use, and nutrient recovery ensure that recovered materials are safe, effective, and accepted in agricultural and industrial applications.

Economic incentives are powerful drivers for investment in resource recovery infrastructure. Grants, tax credits, low-interest loans, and subsidies help offset the costs of establishing composting facilities, anaerobic digesters, or advanced recycling plants. Fee structures that make landfill disposal more expensive than recovery alternatives further encourage the adoption of circular practices.

Policies that support research and development accelerate innovation in recovery technologies and systems. Funding for pilot projects, demonstration sites, and cross-sector partnerships enables the testing and scaling of new approaches. Knowledge sharing platforms and technical assistance programs help disseminate best practices and build capacity among stakeholders.

EPR schemes and product stewardship policies require manufacturers, retailers, and food service providers to take responsibility for the end-of-life management of their products and packaging. This creates demand for resource-efficient design, recovery systems, and closed-loop supply chains.

Collaborative governance—bringing together public agencies, industry groups, academic institutions, and community organizations—ensures that policies are well-informed, practical, and inclusive. Ongoing stakeholder engagement helps refine regulations, address challenges, and respond to emerging opportunities.

With a supportive policy landscape, food systems can unlock the full potential of resource recovery. These policies help build resilient, circular economies where waste is minimized, resources are regenerated, and sustainability is embedded at every level.

Integrating Resource Recovery in Urban and Rural Contexts

Integrating resource recovery into both urban and rural contexts is essential for building circular food systems that are adaptable, inclusive, and sustainable. While the principles of circularity are shared, the strategies, challenges, and opportunities for resource recovery differ based on the unique characteristics of urban and rural environments.

In urban areas, high population density, concentrated waste generation, and well-developed infrastructure provide opportunities for centralized resource recovery systems. Municipal composting facilities, anaerobic digesters, and recycling centers can process large volumes of food and organic waste collected from households, restaurants, markets, and food service providers. Urban agriculture projects, rooftop gardens, and community gardens create demand for recovered compost and nutrients, closing loops within the city. Cities also benefit from digital technologies and logistics platforms that enable efficient collection, data tracking, and redistribution of surplus food.

Challenges in urban settings include logistical complexities, regulatory requirements, and the need for public engagement to ensure effective participation in source separation and recycling programs. Space constraints may limit on-site processing options, requiring investments in collection and transport systems to move materials to centralized facilities. Policy support and strong public-private partnerships are key to overcoming these barriers and scaling up resource recovery.

Rural contexts, on the other hand, are characterized by dispersed populations, proximity to agricultural activities, and often, a greater reliance on natural resource-based livelihoods. On-farm composting, nutrient recycling, and small-scale biogas systems are practical and cost-effective solutions in rural areas. Agricultural residues, livestock manure, and food processing by-products can be processed and reused locally, enriching soils and supporting sustainable farming practices.

Resource recovery in rural settings supports closed-loop agriculture, reduces dependency on external inputs, and helps farmers manage waste responsibly. Collaborative models—such as cooperatives or community resource centers—can aggregate waste from multiple farms or villages for shared processing and value creation.

Bridging urban and rural resource flows is an emerging opportunity. Surplus food, organic waste, and recovered nutrients can move between city and countryside, creating synergies that benefit both settings. Regional networks and integrated planning help optimize resource allocation, reduce waste, and support the development of resilient food systems.

By tailoring resource recovery strategies to the specific needs and assets of urban and rural contexts, communities unlock the full benefits of circularity, improving sustainability, economic opportunity, and environmental health across diverse landscapes.

Chapter 8: Governance, Policy, and Financing Circular Food Systems

Effective governance, supportive policies, and robust financing mechanisms are essential for scaling the circular food economy. This chapter delves into the roles of multilevel governance, policy instruments, and regulatory approaches that guide and accelerate circularity across the food system. It examines economic incentives, innovative investment models, monitoring and verification frameworks, and the significance of international collaboration and public-private partnerships. By aligning strategies, mobilizing resources, and fostering stakeholder engagement, governance and finance structures create the foundation for lasting transformation toward sustainable, resilient, and circular food systems.

Multilevel Governance for Circular Food Economy

Multilevel governance is critical for advancing the circular food economy, ensuring that policies, strategies, and actions are aligned across local, regional, national, and international levels. This coordinated approach recognizes the complexity of food systems and the need for collaboration among a wide range of actors—governments, businesses, civil society, and communities—to drive meaningful change.

At the local level, city councils, municipal agencies, and community organizations are often responsible for implementing circular food initiatives. These can include waste separation and collection programs, support for urban agriculture, and incentives for local composting or food redistribution. Local authorities are well-placed to understand community needs, tailor solutions, and engage residents in circular practices.

Regional governance bodies help bridge the gap between local actions and national policies. Regional networks facilitate resource sharing, infrastructure development, and best-practice exchange among cities and rural areas. By coordinating planning and investment, regions can develop integrated food systems that efficiently manage waste, recover resources, and foster resilient supply chains.

National governments play a central role in establishing legal frameworks, setting targets, and providing funding for circular economy transitions. They create the regulatory environment that enables circular food systems, develop standards for resource recovery, and align incentives for businesses and consumers. National strategies often include education campaigns, research funding, and the integration of circularity into agricultural, environmental, and economic policies.

International organizations and agreements further shape the direction of circular food economies. The United Nations, the European Union, and other multilateral bodies facilitate cooperation, set shared goals, and support knowledge exchange across countries. Global standards and reporting frameworks encourage harmonized approaches and track progress toward sustainability targets.

Effective multilevel governance requires mechanisms for coordination, dialogue, and joint decision-making. Cross-sector partnerships, stakeholder forums, and participatory processes ensure that diverse perspectives are considered and that actions are both practical and equitable. Regular monitoring and evaluation provide feedback for continuous improvement and accountability.

By fostering collaboration and coherence across governance levels, food systems are better equipped to implement circular solutions, respond to local and global challenges, and scale innovations. Multilevel governance underpins a successful transition to the circular food economy, promoting sustainability, resilience, and shared prosperity for all.

Policy Instruments and Regulatory Approaches

Policy instruments and regulatory approaches play a pivotal role in steering the food system toward circularity, setting the rules, incentives, and frameworks that enable sustainable practices across the value chain. By combining mandatory measures with voluntary initiatives, governments can address market failures, remove barriers to circularity, and stimulate innovation.

Command-and-control regulations set clear requirements for food producers, processors, retailers, and consumers. Examples include bans or restrictions on landfilling biodegradable waste, mandates for separate collection and recycling of organics, and minimum recycled content standards for packaging. Food waste reduction targets, mandatory reporting, and eco-design regulations drive compliance and accountability throughout the sector.

Economic instruments provide powerful incentives for stakeholders to adopt circular practices. Subsidies, tax credits, and grants support investment in technologies such as composting, anaerobic digestion, or resource recovery infrastructure. Landfill taxes and pay-as-you-throw schemes create cost differentials that make waste prevention and recycling financially attractive compared to disposal. Deposit-refund systems encourage the return and reuse of packaging, while EPR policies require companies to manage the end-of-life impacts of their products.

Voluntary agreements, certification schemes, and industry standards complement regulatory approaches. These initiatives enable businesses to commit to waste reduction, sustainable sourcing, or resource-efficient packaging. Public recognition, eco-labels, and circular economy certifications enhance market differentiation and build consumer trust. Partnerships between government, industry, and civil society foster collaboration, share best practices, and mobilize collective action.

Information-based instruments, such as public awareness campaigns, transparent reporting, and product labeling, empower consumers to make informed choices and support circular practices. Education and training programs build capacity for compliance and innovation across the sector.

Integrated regulatory frameworks ensure that circular economy policies are aligned with broader objectives in agriculture, waste management, climate action, and economic development. Regular monitoring and evaluation of policy impacts allow for continuous improvement and adaptation to emerging challenges.

By deploying a mix of policy instruments and regulatory approaches, governments can create an enabling environment for circular food systems. These measures guide the transition away from linear models, unlocking economic, environmental, and social benefits for current and future generations.

Economic Incentives and Financing Mechanisms

Economic incentives and financing mechanisms are central to accelerating the adoption of circular practices across the food system. By reducing financial barriers and rewarding sustainable behaviors, these tools encourage investment in innovations that minimize waste, optimize resource use, and close material loops.

Subsidies, tax credits, and grants are among the most direct forms of economic support for circular food initiatives. Governments may provide financial assistance for the installation of composting facilities, anaerobic digesters, or resource recovery technologies, helping to offset high upfront costs. Grants can also fund research and pilot projects that test new approaches to circularity, accelerating the development and scaling of solutions.

Preferential loans and green bonds offer attractive financing terms for businesses pursuing circular projects. Low-interest loans, loan guarantees, or dedicated credit lines reduce the cost of capital for investments in equipment, infrastructure, or business model innovation. Green bonds enable companies or municipalities to raise funds from investors for projects with verified environmental benefits, such as waste reduction, renewable energy generation, or sustainable packaging.

Pay-as-you-throw schemes and landfill taxes are economic instruments that shift costs toward waste generation, creating a financial incentive for households and businesses to prevent, reuse, or recycle waste. Deposit-refund systems reward consumers for returning packaging or products for reuse or recycling, supporting closed-loop supply chains and reducing litter.

EPR policies incorporate economic incentives by requiring manufacturers and retailers to fund the collection, recycling, or proper disposal of their products. This shifts costs away from taxpayers and encourages companies to design products and packaging for circularity from the outset.

Public procurement policies that favor suppliers with strong circular credentials stimulate market demand for sustainable products and services. This approach can help build economies of scale for circular solutions, making them more accessible and affordable.

Innovative financing mechanisms, such as impact investing and blended finance, are gaining traction in the circular economy. These approaches combine public, private, and philanthropic capital to support high-impact projects, reduce risk, and mobilize additional resources.

Through the strategic use of economic incentives and financing mechanisms, stakeholders across the food system can unlock investment, scale up circular practices, and drive the transformation toward a more sustainable, resilient, and resource-efficient future.

Monitoring, Reporting, and Verification

Monitoring, reporting, and verification (MRV) are essential components for advancing circularity in food systems. These processes provide the transparency, accountability, and data-driven insights needed to track progress, ensure compliance, and inform continuous improvement across the value chain.

Effective monitoring begins with the systematic collection of data on resource flows, waste generation, emissions, and other key performance indicators. Digital tools, such as sensors, inventory management systems, and real-time analytics, allow businesses, policymakers, and researchers to capture detailed information on the inputs and outputs of food production, processing, distribution, and consumption. Standardized data collection protocols ensure consistency and comparability, making it possible to benchmark performance and identify best practices.

Regular reporting translates raw data into actionable information for stakeholders. Clear, accessible reports communicate progress toward targets—such as reductions in food waste, increased recycling rates, or lower greenhouse gas emissions. Public disclosure builds trust with consumers, investors, and partners, and enables collaboration across the sector. Many regulatory frameworks require businesses to report on sustainability performance, while voluntary reporting standards, such as those set by the Global Reporting Initiative (GRI), encourage broader participation and transparency.

Verification provides confidence that reported data is accurate, reliable, and in compliance with established standards or regulations. Independent audits, third-party certifications, and on-site inspections validate reported outcomes and guard against greenwashing or misrepresentation. Verification processes can also uncover areas for improvement, inform policy adjustments, and enhance stakeholder credibility.

MRV systems should be designed for adaptability and learning. As technologies evolve and new metrics emerge, organizations can refine their approaches, update targets, and align efforts with evolving best practices and stakeholder expectations.

Robust monitoring, reporting, and verification practices enable food systems to track their progress toward circularity, demonstrate impact, and build momentum for further change. This evidence-based approach supports effective decision-making, resource allocation, and the scaling of circular solutions throughout the sector.

The Role of International Collaboration

International collaboration is a driving force in advancing the circular food economy, enabling countries, organizations, and stakeholders to share knowledge, align strategies, and address shared challenges on a global scale. As food systems are inherently interconnected—spanning supply chains, markets, and resource flows across borders—collaborative action amplifies impact and accelerates the transition to circularity worldwide.

Multilateral organizations, such as the United Nations (UN), FAO, and the World Bank, play key roles in facilitating dialogue, building consensus, and supporting coordinated action. Global agreements and frameworks, like the Sustainable Development Goals (SDGs), set shared objectives for food waste reduction, sustainable production, and responsible consumption, guiding national policies and investments toward circularity.

International research partnerships foster innovation by connecting leading academic institutions, technology developers, and practitioners. Joint projects and knowledge-sharing platforms support the adaptation and scaling of best practices, from precision agriculture and resource recovery to food waste prevention and surplus redistribution. Collaborative initiatives help countries access expertise, technical assistance, and financial resources needed to build circular capacity.

Trade and regulatory harmonization are essential for scaling circular food systems globally. Aligning standards for food safety, resource recovery, eco-labeling, and packaging facilitates cross-border exchange of products and materials, reduces market barriers, and promotes circular supply chains. International standards bodies, such as the International Organization for Standardization (ISO), help create a level playing field and build trust among trading partners.

International collaboration also supports capacity building in developing countries, where access to infrastructure, finance, and technology may be limited. Through technical assistance, funding mechanisms, and South-South cooperation, partners can help bridge gaps and ensure that circular economy benefits are shared equitably.

Joint action is especially important in responding to transboundary challenges—such as climate change, biodiversity loss, and resource scarcity—that require coordinated solutions. By working together, countries and organizations accelerate learning, reduce duplication of effort, and create momentum for policy innovation.

International collaboration strengthens food system resilience, spreads the benefits of circularity, and supports the achievement of sustainability goals on a global scale.

Public-Private Partnerships and Investment Models

Public-private partnerships (PPPs) and innovative investment models are vital for scaling circular solutions in the food system. By bringing together the strengths and resources of government, business, and civil society, these collaborative arrangements can drive innovation, mobilize funding, and accelerate the adoption of circular practices across the value chain.

PPPs leverage the complementary capabilities of public and private sector actors. Governments offer policy support, regulatory frameworks, and access to funding or incentives, while businesses contribute technical expertise, operational capacity, and market access. Civil society organizations often provide local knowledge, stakeholder engagement, and monitoring functions. By aligning goals and sharing risks, PPPs can address challenges that are too complex or costly for any one sector to tackle alone.

Investment models tailored to the circular food economy help direct capital toward impactful projects. Blended finance combines public, private, and philanthropic funding to reduce risk, attract commercial investment, and enable projects that may not otherwise secure financing. Green bonds, sustainability-linked loans, and impact investing instruments are increasingly used to fund circular initiatives such as food waste recovery, resource-efficient infrastructure, or sustainable supply chains.

Incubators and accelerators play a significant role in supporting early-stage startups and small businesses developing circular solutions. These platforms offer seed funding, mentorship, and access to networks, enabling entrepreneurs to test, refine, and scale their innovations. Venture capital and corporate investment provide additional funding for businesses with proven models and strong growth potential.

PPP frameworks often establish clear roles, performance metrics, and shared accountability, ensuring that all partners remain focused on long-term outcomes. Transparent governance and stakeholder engagement build trust and support alignment around common objectives.

Public procurement policies can be used strategically to stimulate demand for circular products and services, creating market opportunities for private sector innovators. Governments and large institutions that prioritize circularity in purchasing decisions set a strong example and help build economies of scale for sustainable solutions.

Collaborative investment approaches also support knowledge sharing and the dissemination of best practices across sectors and regions. Successful projects provide models that can be replicated or adapted in different contexts, accelerating the broader transition to a circular food economy.

Through PPPs and innovative investment models, stakeholders unlock new sources of capital, reduce barriers to adoption, and drive systemic change, enabling food systems to become more sustainable, resilient, and circular.

Overcoming Barriers and Scaling Solutions

Successfully transitioning to a circular food economy involves recognizing and addressing barriers while creating pathways to scale effective solutions. Despite growing momentum for circularity, various technical, financial, regulatory, and cultural challenges can slow progress across the food value chain.

One of the main barriers is the persistence of linear business models and entrenched practices. Companies may be hesitant to adopt new approaches due to perceived risks, uncertainty about returns on investment, or a lack of awareness of circular opportunities. Limited access to finance, especially for small and medium-sized enterprises, further constrains the ability to invest in circular technologies, infrastructure, or training.

Regulatory environments can present challenges when existing laws and standards do not align with circular objectives. Fragmented policies, inconsistent definitions, or restrictive regulations can create uncertainty or even discourage innovative practices. Coordinated policy reforms and regulatory harmonization are necessary to create a level playing field and unlock new opportunities.

Technical and logistical hurdles also impede circularity. Insufficient infrastructure for waste collection, processing, and redistribution—particularly in rural or low-income areas—can limit resource recovery. Gaps in knowledge and capacity make it difficult for businesses and communities to implement circular solutions at scale.

Cultural and behavioral factors, including consumer habits and social norms, shape demand for circular products and services. Resistance to change, lack of information, or unfamiliarity with circular practices can slow adoption at both individual and organizational levels.

To overcome these barriers, targeted interventions are needed. Capacity building and education programs empower stakeholders to understand and adopt circular approaches. Demonstration projects, pilot initiatives, and knowledge-sharing platforms showcase successful models, build confidence, and encourage replication. Financial incentives, grants, and innovative investment mechanisms provide the capital required for scaling.

Public-private partnerships and multi-stakeholder collaborations foster alignment, pool resources, and address complex challenges collectively. Policy reforms and supportive regulation lay the groundwork for systemic change and help drive demand for circular solutions.

Continuous monitoring, reporting, and evaluation ensure that progress is tracked and lessons are integrated into future strategies. As solutions are refined and scaled, food systems move closer to realizing the full benefits of circularity—greater resource efficiency, resilience, and sustainability for communities and the environment.

Chapter 9: Scaling Circular Food Economy for the Future

Scaling the circular food economy for the future requires ambition, innovation, and coordinated action at every level of the food system. This chapter explores pathways for integrating circularity across entire value chains, leveraging digital transformation, and building resilient, adaptive food systems. It highlights the importance of education, workforce development, and broad stakeholder engagement in sustaining momentum and embedding change. Strategies for measuring impact, sharing best practices, and overcoming barriers are discussed, charting a course for global adoption. Through continuous collaboration and learning, food systems can achieve circularity on a scale that benefits people and the planet for generations to come.

Integrating Circularity Across Food Value Chains

Integrating circularity across food value chains involves reimagining every stage of production, processing, distribution, consumption, and end-of-life management to minimize waste, retain value, and regenerate natural systems. Achieving this transformation requires holistic thinking, cross-sector collaboration, and a commitment to continuous improvement throughout the food system.

At the production stage, farmers and primary producers adopt regenerative and resource-efficient practices that restore soil health, enhance biodiversity, and close nutrient cycles. Selecting diverse crop varieties, using precision agriculture technologies, and valorizing agricultural residues ensure that resources are used efficiently and environmental impacts are minimized. On-farm composting and nutrient recycling connect agricultural activities to the broader resource loop.

Processing and manufacturing operations embrace circularity by maximizing the use of all inputs and minimizing waste.

Technologies such as advanced sorting, extraction, and fermentation recover valuable compounds from by-products and side streams. Wastewater and energy recovery systems enable the reuse of water and the generation of renewable energy, reducing the sector's reliance on virgin inputs and fossil fuels.

Distribution and logistics systems are optimized to maintain product quality, reduce spoilage, and facilitate the return and redistribution of surplus or near-expiry goods. Reusable, recyclable, or compostable packaging solutions reduce material waste, while digital platforms enable real-time tracking, demand forecasting, and coordinated inventory management across the supply chain.

Retailers play a central role in driving circularity through efficient inventory management, product innovations, and partnerships with food rescue organizations. Initiatives such as bulk sales, refill stations, and surplus redistribution platforms help extend product life cycles and keep edible food out of waste streams.

Consumer engagement is essential for the success of circular value chains. Education campaigns, digital tools, and community initiatives empower households to plan meals, reduce waste, and participate in recycling or composting programs. Feedback mechanisms enable consumers to influence product design and sustainability initiatives.

End-of-life management prioritizes resource recovery through composting, anaerobic digestion, and recycling, transforming waste into new materials, energy, or soil amendments. Policymakers, businesses, and civil society collaborate to create enabling environments for innovation, investment, and the scaling of circular solutions.

When circularity is integrated at every stage of the food value chain, food systems become more resilient, efficient, and sustainable—benefiting producers, businesses, consumers, and the environment alike.

Leveraging Digital Transformation and Innovation

Digital transformation and innovation are powerful enablers for advancing circularity within food systems. Emerging technologies offer new tools and approaches for optimizing resource use, minimizing waste, and connecting stakeholders throughout the value chain, accelerating the shift toward a more resilient and sustainable food economy.

Advanced data analytics and artificial intelligence (AI) are revolutionizing how food systems operate. AI-powered forecasting tools analyze vast amounts of historical and real-time data to predict demand, optimize harvest schedules, and streamline inventory management, reducing surplus and waste. Machine learning algorithms identify patterns in resource flows, helping businesses pinpoint inefficiencies and target interventions where they have the greatest impact.

IoT devices and smart sensors provide continuous monitoring of environmental conditions, equipment performance, and product quality. In agriculture, soil moisture sensors and weather stations enable precision irrigation and input application, conserving resources while maintaining yields. In processing and logistics, IoT devices track temperature, humidity, and location, safeguarding food safety and extending shelf life.

Blockchain technology is driving transparency and traceability across supply chains. Secure, decentralized ledgers record every transaction and movement of goods, allowing stakeholders to verify origin, production methods, and sustainability credentials. This transparency builds trust among consumers, regulators, and business partners, supporting responsible sourcing and circular practices.

Digital platforms and mobile applications connect producers, processors, retailers, and consumers, enabling efficient resource sharing, surplus redistribution, and secondary market development. Apps that facilitate food sharing, recovery, and donation streamline the movement of edible food to those who need it, reducing waste and supporting food security.

Collaborative platforms and knowledge-sharing networks accelerate the diffusion of best practices and innovations. Digital tools for remote training, virtual workshops, and peer-to-peer learning make it easier for stakeholders to access the information and skills needed to implement circular solutions.

Investment in digital transformation also drives innovation in packaging, logistics, and product development. 3D printing, for example, is being explored for creating customized packaging and tools with minimal material use and waste.

Leveraging digital transformation and innovation empowers food systems to operate more efficiently, responsively, and sustainably. The continued adoption and integration of these technologies will be central to realizing the full potential of the circular food economy and ensuring long-term food system resilience.

Building Resilient and Adaptive Food Systems

Building resilient and adaptive food systems is vital for navigating the uncertainties and complexities of a changing world. Resilience in food systems refers to their ability to withstand shocks—such as extreme weather, market volatility, or disruptions in supply chains—and to recover and adapt in ways that sustain productivity, food security, and environmental health.

Circular food economies provide a strong foundation for resilience by diversifying resource flows, reducing dependency on external inputs, and embedding flexibility into production, processing, and distribution. Diverse cropping systems, regenerative agriculture, and integrated livestock management buffer against pests, diseases, and climate extremes, while also improving soil health and ecosystem services.

Adaptive processing and logistics support resilience by enabling rapid adjustments to shifting supply and demand. Technologies such as real-time data analytics, automated inventory management, and predictive logistics platforms empower businesses to respond proactively to disruptions. Flexible processing facilities, decentralized storage, and shared logistics hubs provide alternatives when central systems face stress or breakdown.

Community engagement and local networks are key for building adaptive capacity. Short supply chains, farmers' markets, and community-supported agriculture create direct connections between producers and consumers, supporting food access during crises. Local food initiatives and mutual aid networks enable resource sharing, surplus redistribution, and collective problem-solving, strengthening social capital and trust.

Policy and governance frameworks must also support resilience and adaptability. Scenario planning, risk assessments, and early warning systems help identify vulnerabilities and guide targeted interventions. Policies that incentivize resource efficiency, circularity, and diversification create a more robust enabling environment for resilient food systems.

Innovation and continuous learning underpin adaptive capacity. Ongoing investment in research, training, and knowledge exchange ensures that stakeholders can adopt new technologies, practices, and strategies in response to emerging challenges. Platforms for sharing best practices and lessons learned facilitate rapid diffusion of successful solutions.

Resilient and adaptive food systems are better equipped to manage risks, capitalize on new opportunities, and ensure food security for all. Integrating circular principles, technological innovation, and community engagement builds systems that are not only sustainable but also flexible and future-ready, capable of thriving amid uncertainty and change.

Education, Training, and Workforce Development

Education, training, and workforce development are fundamental for enabling the circular food economy and ensuring its long-term success. As food systems transition from linear to circular models, new knowledge, skills, and mindsets are required at every level—from production and processing to distribution, retail, and resource recovery.

Formal education plays a key role in preparing the next generation of food system leaders. Integrating circular economy principles, sustainability, and systems thinking into school and university curricula helps students understand the interconnectedness of food, resources, and the environment. Hands-on experiences such as school gardens, composting projects, and community partnerships foster practical skills and an appreciation for resource stewardship.

Vocational training and continuing education are vital for upskilling the existing workforce. Farmers, food processors, logistics providers, and retail staff benefit from targeted programs on regenerative agriculture, efficient processing technologies, waste minimization, and digital tools for resource management. Workshops, certifications, and on-the-job training ensure that workers can adapt to new practices and evolving regulatory requirements.

Specialized training in areas such as resource recovery, waste auditing, or the maintenance of advanced technologies supports the growth of green jobs and circular business models. Partnerships with industry, academic institutions, and government agencies help align training content with labor market needs and emerging trends.

Leadership development and change management training equip managers and decision-makers to guide organizations through the transition to circularity. Building awareness of the business case for circular practices and providing tools for strategic planning and stakeholder engagement foster a culture of innovation and continuous improvement.

Public awareness campaigns, community workshops, and digital learning platforms make education and training accessible to diverse audiences, bridging gaps and supporting inclusion.

Investing in education, training, and workforce development ensures that all stakeholders have the capacity and confidence to implement circular solutions. This foundation of knowledge and skills accelerates the adoption of sustainable practices, supports economic opportunity, and empowers food systems to evolve and thrive in a rapidly changing world.

Engaging Stakeholders Across the Ecosystem

Engaging stakeholders across the food system ecosystem is essential for advancing the circular food economy. The interconnected nature of food systems means that real change relies on the active participation and collaboration of a diverse array of actors—including producers, processors, retailers, consumers, policymakers, researchers, technology providers, financial institutions, and civil society.

A multi-stakeholder approach ensures that circular initiatives are informed by a wide range of perspectives, expertise, and needs. Early and ongoing engagement allows stakeholders to co-design strategies, identify opportunities, and anticipate challenges, fostering shared ownership and buy-in. This collaborative process also enhances the relevance and effectiveness of solutions, as they are tailored to local contexts and stakeholder priorities.

Producers and primary processors are often the starting point for circular transformation, as their practices directly influence resource flows and waste generation. Engaging these actors involves providing training, technical support, and incentives to adopt regenerative agriculture, efficient processing, and waste minimization techniques. Collaboration among farmers, cooperatives, and input suppliers supports knowledge sharing and the development of circular business models.

Retailers and food service providers play a critical role as intermediaries, shaping consumer choices, product design, and the flow of goods and packaging. Engaging these stakeholders includes partnerships for surplus food redistribution, adoption of sustainable packaging, and implementation of take-back or refill schemes.

Consumers are pivotal in driving demand for circular products and services. Education campaigns, digital engagement, and feedback mechanisms empower individuals and communities to reduce waste, choose sustainably, and participate in recycling and composting programs.

Policy and regulatory stakeholders set the enabling framework for circular food systems. Regular dialogue and consultation ensure that policies reflect the realities and needs of all actors, while cross-sectoral task forces and advisory committees foster coordinated action.

Engagement with researchers, technology providers, and financial institutions supports the development, scaling, and financing of innovative circular solutions. Pilots, demonstration projects, and public-private partnerships facilitate experimentation, evaluation, and replication of successful models.

Civil society organizations contribute valuable advocacy, outreach, and monitoring, ensuring that circularity efforts are inclusive and equitable.

Sustained stakeholder engagement creates momentum for change, builds trust, and unlocks the collective intelligence and resources needed to transform food systems. Through inclusive collaboration, circular food economies can achieve lasting impact, resilience, and shared value for all participants.

Measuring Impact and Success

Measuring impact and success is critical for the effective implementation and scaling of circular food economy initiatives. Clear, consistent metrics provide the evidence needed to assess progress, inform decision-making, and demonstrate value to stakeholders across the food system.

Impact measurement begins with the selection of relevant indicators that capture the key outcomes of circular strategies. Common metrics include reductions in food waste, resource use efficiency (water, energy, and materials), greenhouse gas emissions avoided, and quantities of nutrients or materials recovered and recycled. Social and economic indicators—such as jobs created, food security improvements, and community engagement—complement environmental measures, offering a holistic view of success.

Data collection and analysis underpin robust measurement. Digital tools, sensors, and management information systems enable the real-time tracking of resource flows, operational efficiency, and waste generation throughout the value chain. Regular audits and reporting cycles ensure that data remains accurate, up to date, and actionable.

Benchmarking performance against established targets or industry standards helps organizations assess progress and identify areas for improvement. Third-party certifications, voluntary standards, and participation in global reporting frameworks enhance credibility and comparability, building trust among partners, investors, and consumers.

Evaluation should not be limited to quantitative results. Qualitative assessment—gathering feedback from stakeholders, capturing lessons learned, and documenting challenges—provides valuable context and supports continuous learning.

Transparency in measurement and reporting fosters accountability, enables informed decision-making, and motivates further action. Sharing results through public reports, dashboards, and stakeholder forums increases visibility and encourages broader participation in circular initiatives.

Continuous improvement is a defining feature of successful circular food economies. Regular review of goals, indicators, and methodologies ensures that impact measurement remains relevant as technologies, policies, and stakeholder expectations evolve.

By systematically measuring impact and success, food system actors can track their contributions, justify investments, and inspire ongoing progress toward a more circular, resilient, and sustainable future.

Pathways to a Global Circular Food Economy

Transitioning to a global circular food economy requires coordinated action, shared vision, and continuous innovation across all levels of the food system. Pathways to achieving this transformation encompass systemic changes in production, consumption, policy, and collaboration, driven by the imperative to conserve resources, reduce waste, and create sustainable value for people and the planet.

A foundational pathway is the widespread adoption of circular production models. Regenerative agriculture, integrated crop-livestock systems, and precision farming enable producers to close nutrient loops, restore soil health, and minimize external inputs. Investments in resource-efficient processing, advanced waste valorization technologies, and the integration of renewable energy sources reduce the environmental impact of food manufacturing and unlock new opportunities for value creation.

Circular supply chains are built on principles of transparency, traceability, and collaboration. Digital technologies such as blockchain, IoT, and data analytics connect stakeholders, optimize logistics, and enable real-time monitoring of resource flows. Secondary markets, surplus redistribution platforms, and reverse logistics systems ensure that edible food, by-products, and packaging are recovered, reused, or recycled wherever possible.

Policy alignment and regulatory support are essential for scaling circular food economies worldwide. National and international frameworks must incentivize waste prevention, resource recovery, and circular business models through supportive regulation, economic incentives, and extended producer responsibility schemes. Harmonizing standards, facilitating trade, and fostering cross-border cooperation accelerate the global diffusion of best practices and innovations.

Consumer engagement and behavior change play a central role in driving demand for sustainable and circular products. Education campaigns, labeling schemes, and accessible information empower individuals and communities to adopt mindful consumption habits, participate in resource recovery initiatives, and support circular brands.

Collaboration across sectors and geographies is vital for overcoming systemic barriers and harnessing collective intelligence. Public-private partnerships, research networks, and multistakeholder platforms facilitate the exchange of knowledge, technology, and finance needed to scale solutions and ensure inclusive participation.

Global pathways to a circular food economy depend on integrating circularity into every stage of the value chain and across all regions. By pursuing these pathways, societies can create food systems that are productive, resilient, and regenerative—capable of meeting the needs of current and future generations while protecting the earth's natural resources.

Conclusion

The journey toward a circular food economy is both urgent and transformative, offering a clear pathway to address the interconnected challenges of resource scarcity, food waste, environmental degradation, and social inequality. As food systems face mounting pressures from population growth, climate change, and shifting consumption patterns, circularity provides a strategic framework for building resilience, sustainability, and long-term prosperity.

Throughout the food value chain, from production to consumption and beyond, circular principles reshape how resources are managed and valued. By designing out waste, keeping materials in use, and regenerating natural systems, food economies can move away from extractive, linear models toward cycles that restore, replenish, and sustain. The adoption of regenerative agricultural practices, efficient processing technologies, and closed-loop water, nutrient, and energy systems exemplifies this shift in mindset and operations.

Integrating circularity across the food system requires a holistic and collaborative approach. No single actor or sector can achieve meaningful transformation alone. Farmers, processors, retailers, consumers, policymakers, researchers, technology providers, and investors must work together, sharing knowledge, aligning incentives, and co-creating solutions tailored to diverse local and regional contexts. Public-private partnerships, multi-stakeholder platforms, and community-driven initiatives are all essential for unlocking innovation, mobilizing resources, and scaling proven models.

Enabling policies and supportive regulatory frameworks create the necessary conditions for change, offering clear targets, incentives, and accountability mechanisms that guide behavior across the value chain. Economic instruments—such as subsidies, grants, green bonds, and extended producer responsibility schemes—make it possible for businesses and communities to invest in new technologies and practices. Education, training, and workforce development ensure that all stakeholders have the skills and capacity to adapt to and thrive within circular systems.

Digital transformation and technological innovation further accelerate the transition, providing powerful tools for real-time data collection, monitoring, traceability, and resource optimization. These advances enable more precise interventions, improve transparency, and facilitate the integration of circular solutions at scale.

Social norms and cultural shifts also play a crucial role. When sustainable consumption, waste reduction, and resource recovery become widely accepted and expected, the circular food economy becomes embedded in daily life. Public awareness campaigns, school programs, and consumer engagement initiatives foster the necessary behavior changes and reinforce community participation.

The benefits of embracing a circular food economy are far-reaching. Circular systems conserve natural resources, reduce greenhouse gas emissions, restore biodiversity, and support healthy soils and water systems. They also enhance food security, create economic opportunities, and build more equitable, inclusive communities. By prioritizing regeneration, resilience, and shared value, the circular food economy lays the foundation for a sustainable future that meets the needs of both people and the planet.

Looking ahead, the global transition to a circular food economy will depend on continued leadership, investment, innovation, and collaboration at every level. With commitment and shared vision, food systems can become engines of regeneration—capable of nourishing humanity while restoring and preserving the natural world for generations to come.

www.ingramcontent.com/pod-product-compliance
Lightning Source LLC
Chambersburg PA
CBHW052139270326
41930CB00012B/2955